BREAKING GROUND
ART, ARCHAEOLOGY & MYTHOLOGY

Colophon

BREAKING GROUND:
ART, ARCHAEOLOGY & MYTHOLOGY

While copyright in the volume as a whole is vested in Axis Projects, copyright in individual texts and memorabilia submissions belongs to their respective owners, and no part of this publication may be reproduced wholly or in part without the express permission in writing of both publisher and owners.

© AP Publishing, the artists, authors
and the memorabilia owners

Published by Axis Projects Publishing
c/o Axis Graphic Design Ltd
www.axisgraphicdesign.co.uk
email: ap@axisgraphicdesign.co.uk

A catalogue record for this book is available from
the British Library

ISBN 978-0-9554825-6-4
A limited edition hardback with dvd of 500 copies

Design: www.axisgraphicdesign.co.uk
Typeset in Quire Sans Pro by Jim Ford, Monotype
'I am John Brodie' set in Scala Sans Pro
Printed in Belgium by Graphius, Ghent

Breaking Ground project was supported by:

  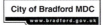

1907 Halfpenny, archaeological find (c043)

Peter Barker, Bradford Park Avenue fan, video still

Joe Mosley

FOREWORD

3 May 1974: Bradford Park Avenue is officially wound up at the Midland Hotel in Bradford.

31 August 1988: Bradford Park Avenue play their first game after reforming as a football club in the thirteenth tier of the English football leagues.

3 May 2004: Promotion is gained to the Football Conference North via the play-offs.

31 August 2016: Bradford Park Avenue Community Football Club is officially launched at the Midland Hotel in Bradford – the first community-owned football club in West Yorkshire.

Bradford Park Avenue FC has a long and very proud history as a football club and as part of the fabric of this city. Over many generations our fans have seen the highs and the lows of the club, the worst of which for our loyal followers was being put out of business in 1974. But since reforming we have fought our way up through the leagues and this next step into community ownership – which has proved to be very successful at several other clubs in the country – should secure the club's future and bring something back to the people of the city. We will be 'Breaking New Ground' as the first club in the county of Yorkshire to make this transition. Putting the club on a more sustainable platform will enhance our status at Horsfall and allow us to plan long-term, developing the ground and facilities as a genuine asset for the local community.

Chief Executive Gareth Roberts said, 'I believe that it's really important that any club can stand on its own feet and be rooted in the community and not rely solely on the whims of a private owner. The club will have a more sustainable future if it is owned and run by local people who are passionate about not only the football – which I hope will flourish – but also about other sports and activities and about investing in relationships with the local community, its schools and local businesses. This has been my ambition for the club for several years. I'm originally a Bradford lad and a long-time fan of the club so I'll still be involved and am willing to put my hand in my pocket to support growth, particularly around community facilities and for initiatives to strengthen our links with the next generation of players and supporters.'

As a club we need as much support as we can get in this exciting time, which brings with it new challenges. That means volunteers helping with whatever skills they feel able to share. It also means extending our fan base and club membership by reaching out into the community and supporting the ambitions of young players and fans.

This book is a timely reminder to new and old fans alike of the rich heritage of Bradford Park Avenue. It is also an example of how collaboration can achieve something uniquely special and is an inspiration as we move forward into community ownership.

Joe Mosley
Bradford Park Avenue Community Football Club
Club and Community Development Director

November 2013: archaeological dig to find the left-hand goalpost hole

In 2013, the Park Avenue football ground, a long-forgotten time capsule of Bradford's social history, began to be unearthed when archaeologist Jason Wood and artist Neville Gabie conducted the first ever archaeological excavation of a football goalmouth and goalpost. This small intervention generated significant interest and was witnessed by people of all ages. Most had stories to tell; many also brought personal memorabilia and photographs to share. All displayed a passion for the former ground and a willingness to see it investigated and utilised to better effect.

Neville Gabie

INTRODUCTION

Jason Wood, David Pendleton and I arrived at the old Bradford Park Avenue football ground on Horton Park Avenue early on a grey November morning in 2013, equipped with an archaeologist's kitbag, enthusiasm, curiosity and no idea of quite what to expect. Our plan was simple – to locate and excavate one of the goalpost holes and some of the goal area at the Horton Park End of this once famous stadium. This was to be the first ever dig (as far as we knew) of a former football ground's goalmouth. We had put out a call, more in hope then expectation, that there would still be fans out there who remained interested in the old club, one of the first genuinely top-flight clubs to fall from grace and abandon its ground when it dropped out of the Football League 40 years earlier. To our genuine surprise during the next few days we were overwhelmed by visitors and supporters, still carrying the flame and cherishing memories intertwined with their own, of youth, hope and loyalty to the colours of 'The Avenue'. Many fought their way through the forest of trees that had replaced them on the still intact concrete terraces; looking for 'their spot' – the place from where they always watched the game. As we set them the task of sweeping away the leaves and debris, the ground gradually revealed itself. As terrace steps appeared so conversations and reminiscences flourished. Leaning on broomsticks and shovels, the Horton Park End once again for the briefest of moments populated with colour, voices and passionate debate about first matches, best games, favourite players.

Invigorated by their enthusiasm, with funding from Arts Council England and the National Football Museum, and with the blessing of Bradford Council, we returned with an expanded team for one week in September 2015. That first experience convinced us that we ought to do a bigger project at Bradford Park Avenue before its legacy was lost forever. We had a vision of doing more archaeology, involving more artists, of uncovering more of those stories.

Jason, David and I were joined by photographer and designer Alan Ward, he contributed as one of the artists onsite, and helping to shape the final delivery of the work. Jason recruited the services of Dr Chris Gaffney, a renowned expert in geophysical surveying from Bradford University, archaeologist Robert Nichols and several archaeology students from the University. We invited artists Oliver Palmer and Giorgio Garippa, and botanical artist Louise O'Reilly to join us. Once again we made public calls for fans and the curious to join us to help with the dig and share their insights and memorabilia. People turned out in their hundreds. Again we were overwhelmed by their personal histories and treasures.

This publication brings together some of that material, but it would have amounted to very little without the generous and passionate contributions of The Avenue fans themselves. It is a publication which uses art and archaeology to celebrate the mythology of this once great club.

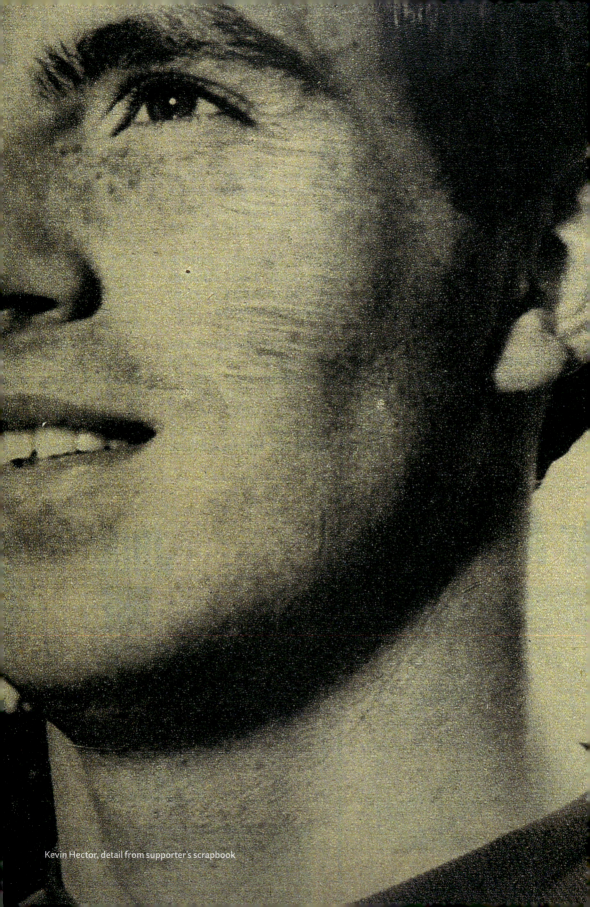

Kevin Hector, detail from supporter's scrapbook

MAWBY & NEAL, 41, KIRKGATE, BRADFORD — No. 2,100 — SATURDAY, 10 JANUARY, 1948

BRADFORD'S MAGNIFICENT CUP-TIE VI[CTORY]

Mighty Arsenal's Form and Reputation Smashed to [Smithereens]

AVENUE'S SUCCESS RICHLY DESERVED

Elliott's Brilliant Goal in First Half

(By "WANDERER")

BRADFORD were in good heart and perfect physical condition for the biggest Cup task they had to face in at the club's 40 years' history.

... the worst they meant ... down fighting against ... Arsenal at High... where only Liver... had conquered the Division leaders this ...

... side they chose last ... duly went into ... and these were the ...

...nal—Swindin; Male, Scott; ... Compton, Mercer; Roper, Lewis, Rooks, McPherson, ...ford—Farr; Hepworth, Farrell; Greenwood, Deplidge, Smith, Ainsley, Downie, Elliott, ... C. J. Barrick (North...

QUEUES AT 10 O'CLOCK

Bradford players, who ... a London theatre last ... were duly impressed ... their first sight of High... where only Ainsley ... had played previously ... found the turf, just a ... soft on top, in splendid ... ion.

...ager Emery had paid a ... to the ground during the ... and returned to ... queues of spec... had formed as early as ... lock.

... saw the Avenue colours ... in evidence among the ... on a cold but fine after ... and there were indica... half an hour before ... that the crowd might ... touch the 60,000 mark.

Avenue players were ... such a thunderous ... ion that one might almost ... imagined that the greater ... tion of the crowd came ... Bradford, and the singing ... kla, Moor Baht 'At" gave ... Yorkshire flavour and ... phere to the event.

BRADFORD HIT BACK

...enwood lost the toss to ..., but there was little ...tage in that. There ... thing evidence about the ... which Bradford went ... effect, but they were ... upon immediately to cope ... Arsenal's right wing ..., in one of which Roper ... out great pace, swept ... Farrell and centred ... fully when on the run ...wis to hit a fierce low ... only a yard wide.

...ford promptly hit back to ... the ball down the left wing ... Elliott dropped across a ... centre, but as Ainsley ... in Swindin came out and ... ed it beautifully to take ... off his head.

... was surprising to see ... and Scott get in each ... way when Bradford ... ade play on the right. ...nith nipped in and left ... of them floundering as ... intercepted his push ...

...RR'S GRAND SAVE

Avenue defenders once ... were inclined to be ... over-eager, and Hep... and Farr hampered each ... once when McPherson ... at hand, but nothing ... developed ... quick succession both ... and Greenwood turned ... into attack by quick and ... footwork, and the ...dings in the first ten ... found Jack as good as ... ster.

... the same only grand ... 'on by Farr saved ... when McPherson's ...onal pace left Hepworth ... in the rear, for the goal... came out at just ... moment and narrowed the ... charging down the shot,

He Scored the Vital Goal

ELLIOTT, Bradford's local born outside-left, whose goal knocked mighty Arsenal out of the cup.

wood was setting an inspiring example to his comrades.

The only shot by either side for a long spell was a long-range effort by Ainsley, which went wide, but it was undignified to see more than one Arsenal defender resorting to a foul in holding off one or other of the Bradford forwards.

Ainsley was once given a possible chance by Downie, but he failed to bring the ball under quick control in the penalty area, and he was beaten to it by Compton, but for whose power Arsenal might easily have been behind by this time.

ARSENAL WORRIED

The rattles made a terrific din when Downie delivered a fierce drive which looked to have goal written all over it, but Swindin made a spectacular diving save in turning it round for another corner, following which Deplidge fired over.

More than half an hour had gone, and worried Arsenal were being repeatedly penned in their own penalty area by the persistent Avenue players, who were making a truly great fight, not merely to save the game but to win it.

Arsenal had other escapes when further shots by Downie and Deplidge were within a foot of the goal.

Could Bradford keep it up? This was the big question, but following a brisk right wing thrust, Downie got in a beautiful header which looked every inch a goal, but Swindin made another superb save.

GOAL FOR BRADFORD

Even then Arsenal were being really run off their feet by this magnificent Avenue light, and they were glad to concede two more corners, with the Bradford forwards repeatedly swarming through.

Following the second of them a goal came at last, as it had threatened for long, for the ball was in the home penalty area for a minute or two before it went out to the left, where ELLIOTT fastened upon it to hit a glorious rising drive of great power which neither Swindin nor any other 'keeper alive could

COLCHESTER SURPRISE

Huddersfield Defeated

SIXTEEN thousand spectators watched Huddersfield Town at Colchester, to-day, play the local club in the third round of the F.A. Cup.

The weather was fine and the ground sticky. The teams were:

Colchester — Wright; Kettle, Allen; Bearman, Fenton, Brown; Hillman, Curry, Turner, Cutting, Carter.

Huddersfield Town — Hesford; Hayes, Barker; Smith (L.), Hepplewhite, Boot; Smith (W. C.), Glazzard, Whittingham, Doherty, Metcalfe.

Referee: Mr. G. Reader.

DOHERTY HURT

Wright kept goal for Colchester, instead of Lamare, who failed a fitness test at the last moment.

In the first few seconds of the game a drive from Curry hit Doherty on the side of the face and the Irish star went down and was obviously shaken. He soon resumed, however, and sent Metcalfe away, but Wright came out and cleared.

The first thrill came when Hesford, worried by Hillman, dropped the ball, but Barker kicked clear.

Colchester were at least holding their own, with Fenton, ex-England international, keeping the Colchester defence steady.

Whittingham headed straight at Wright from Glazzard's cross and Allen cleared another Town attack.

DEFENCE NOT SOUND

Colchester were obviously taking no notice of anybody's reputation, and Turner had a fine drive well saved by Hesford, who turned the ball just wide of the posts.

The Huddersfield defence was anything but sound, and twice Barker miskicked under pressure.

The other kick, taken by Kettle, was beautifully cleared by Hesford, and Berryman twice stopped Metcalfe at the other end.

From a Metcalfe corner Glazzard headed straight at Lamare.

GOOD DEFENCE

There was nothing in the play to show any disparity in class at this stage.

A tremendous drive from Turner was blocked by his skipper, Curry, and a Colchester corner was headed clear by Hepplewhite.

Colchester's first-time defensive measures did not allow of any tricky football from Doherty and company.

Colchester forced two corners, and from the second Fenton headed over.

Wright, in the Colchester goal, hardly had a shot to save, so effectively did Fenton, Kettle and Allen cover and clear.

Just before half-time Turner raced through and shot wide.

Half-time: Colchester 0gl., Huddersfield T. 0gl.

It was obvious the narrowness of the pitch was affecting the Huddersfield men.

From a clever Doherty opening Metcalfe shot over, and then Doherty netted, but was pulled up for "hands."

After 24 minutes Colchester took the lead. Allen put in a terrific free-kick which was punched out by Hesford to the feet of CURRY, who shot straight in at point-blank range.

Three minutes later Turner went through and scored but off-side was given.

Huddersfield put in a tremendous rally, but the Colchester defence, with Kettle outstanding, never faulted.

When the final whistle went the crowd broke the barriers and each man of the Colchester team was carried shoulder high from the ground.

Result: Colchester 1, Huddersfield T. 0.

"Sports" photographers were on Rugby League grounds to-day—Odsal and Featherstone Rovers, and the incidents in the top two pictures are of D. W... (Featherstone) being tackled by Kitching. Below is shown a scramble for an opponent in a...

FEW BRIGHT SPOTS AT ODSAL STADIUM

Featherstone Weak Foes For Bradford Northern

(By "THE ORACLE")

FEATHERSTONE ROVERS, who visited Odsal Stadium this afternoon, have never beaten Bradford Northern in a cup or league game on this ground.

The Rovers have not gained a victory for over two months, and have only won five games this season.

Bradford Northern made two changes, Walters coming in for Batten, and Tyler displaced Orford in the second row. Waring returned to the Featherstone threequarter line. Teams:

Bradford Northern.—Carmichael; Walters, Kitching, Ward (R.), Edwards; Davies, Ward (D.); Whitcombe, Darlison, Greaves, Tyler, Foster and Traill.

Featherstone Rovers.—Norbury; Crabtree, Waring, Tennant, Gunn; Allman, Russell; Ramskill, Mogg, Pawson, Allinson, Garner and Richardson.

Referee: Mr. L. J. Barker.

A crowd of about 5,000 saw Northern take up the offensive, due to bad handling by the Rovers' backs.

After only two minutes Bradford took the lead, when DONALD WARD received the for a run up the middle, for when the ball reached Davies from a cunning reverse pass from Kitching, he was well covered.

Another try should have come Northern's way after 35 minutes, when Walters made another run, but when near the line he had no support, and was tackled in possession.

A minute later Northern did manage to penetrate their opponents' line again, following a splendid passing bout. The ball swung among the three-quarters before EDWARDS finished off the move with a touch-down in the corner. E. WARD did not convert.

A crowd of about 5,000 saw Northern take up the offensive, due to bad handling by the Rovers' backs.

A wild wily passing by the Bradford backs gave Featherstone an opportunity. CRABTREE picked up the ball, and outpaced all his challengers in a thrilling 40-yard run for a try, which NORBURY converted.

SURPRISE FOR HALIFAX

CLEVER PLAY BY WORKINGTON TOWN

(By "BEACON")

The appearance of recently signed Maori Kia Rika and the return of Arthur Bassett to the Halifax threequarter line stiffened appearance for teams home encounter Workington.

Peter Gronow on a trial with Halifax from Huddersfield displaced Mawson among the forwards.

Workington had one change, Hodgson replacing Miller, who moved over in the forwards to occupy Waring's position. Teams:

Halifax.—Taylor; Daniels, Rika, Bassett, Ward Keilty; Meek, Flowers, Smith, Greenwood, H.

Workington.—Risman; Alker (J. H.), Rogers, Carr (R.); Pepperill; Hughes, Ackerley, Miller, Park, Iveson.

Referee: Mr. P. Cowell, Warrington.

... were about present when Keilty kicked for Halifax, and almost a dangerous situation for Workington was opened. Daniels, who came in scoring with a long run took him close to the ...

It was back in 1966 that a neighbour was badgering me to come along to Bradford Park Avenue, extolling the virtues of what turned out to be the great Kevin Hector. My long-lasting memory is of entering the ground at the Canterbury Avenue end, and of going up some wooden railway sleeper steps to get to the back of the Kop. What unfolded was this magnificent stadium in early September, beautifully painted in the club colours – a Racing Green. The grass was manicured, the walls around the pitch whitewashed, and the whole spectacle was just inspiring for a young ten year old.

I was lucky enough to be a ball-boy from 1966 to 1970. We found ourselves changing in the boiler room, just at the entrance to the pitch from the old Dolls House. Over time I became quite attached to the club badge sewn onto a remnant of a green shirt, which I later found out was the away kit from the 65-66 season. After some time I finally found the courage to ask the boiler man if I could unpick the badge from the shirt, which by then was just used as a rag to clean the boiler. I have kept the badge ever since.

Mike Stead

I missed the ball hitting the back of the net! I watched kick-off just as I was going down the few steps under the dressing-room to pitch 'bridge' and heard the roar before I got up the other side.

Dave Towning

Jim Fryatt's goal for Bradford Park Avenue versus Tranmere, 25 April 1964

According to the sources some onlookers say that this goal took closer to 10 seconds. However there is no film evidence to contradict the assessment of the referee Bob Simons who said: 'I blew my whistle for the start and still had my stopwatch in my hand when the ball entered the net. The scoring time is exactly four seconds – no question of it.'

Wikipedia: Fastest goals in association football

OFFICIAL PROGRAMME

BRADFORD PARK AVENUE A.F.C.

PRICE 3ᴰ

At Park Avenue   Football League Div. 3 (North)

BRADFORD CITY

Saturday, October 12th.   Kick-off 3-0 p.m.

AUSTIN RETAIL DEALERS   ALL MAKES OF CARS SUPPLIED

BAYLEY MOTOR CO.

(Prop. ALAN PICKLES)

DUDLEY HILL, BRADFORD 4
Telephone: DUDLEY HILL 61

—SALES REPAIRS AND ALL SERVICES—

FOR COMPLETE RESULTS YOU MUST GET

YORKSHIRE SPORTS

EVERY SATURDAY NIGHT

THE COMPLETE SPORTS PAPER

David Pendleton

BRADFORD PARK AVENUE
A HISTORICAL AND CULTURAL OVERVIEW

Bradford Park Avenue. Once a rival to Headingley and Bramall Lane in a Victorian battle for sporting supremacy in the White Rose county. Underneath the mock-Tudor pavilion the sound of willow on leather spoke of the lazy cricketing days of summer, while next door beneath the triple gables of the main football stand, as autumn turned to winter, the football codes entertained the mill hand and the mill owner alike. For a few glorious decades, particularly prior to the tragedy of the Great War, the Park Avenue grounds must have had a sense of permanence and timelessness. As tens of thousands craned their necks to catch every twist and turn of sporting drama, few could have envisaged that by the ground's centenary the shouts and cries of the crowds would be but a fading memory as the grounds fell into a state of dereliction. For many decades there was an air of melancholy about the semi-abandoned Park Avenue grounds. However, today the history of the site is being revisited and re-evaluated. As Park Avenue approaches its 140th birthday archaeologists, artists, historians and even botanists are busy disturbing the old ghosts. Reawakening memories and reminding people that Park Avenue is still a special place in the context of the sporting and leisure culture of Bradford and beyond.

Despite the multi-sport nature of Park Avenue it is arguably the footballing heritage that dominates how the site is remembered and perceived. This is partly explained by the strong connection between the architecture used to embellish the football ground and its use in constructing a sense of place that still lingers four decades after the last ball was kicked. Although the stands have long succumbed to the demolition man, the gables of the main stand and the 'Dolls House' changing rooms still resonate strongly in the self-image of Bradford (Park Avenue) AFC. There can be few other football clubs where the architecture of the home ground has had such a lasting impact. While such an attachment can be partly explained by nostalgia and melancholy for lost status and even the youth of those remembering, it has to be acknowledged that Park Avenue was never a run of the mill football ground. With its back-to-back football and cricket stand, soaring gables surmounted by the city coat of arms, the Dolls House with architectural echoes of the neighbouring cricket pavilion, the very fabric of Park Avenue resonated with a sense of history and tradition that often jarred with the travails of the football club during its later years.

The question has to be asked, did the grand architecture of Park Avenue represent a lost greatness or was it an ongoing attempt to invent a tradition and status? To answer that quandary we must delve in the deep history of the grounds and travel back to a period when Bradford was the rapidly expanding 'worstedopolis', or wool capital of the world. The Park Avenue grounds were developed in 1880 by an amalgamation of Bradford Cricket Club and Bradford Rugby Club. The fortunes of the cricket club, formalised in 1836 but active from at least 1832, are almost representative of the wider city – or town as it was then. The club was forced to vacate two home grounds due to the development of middle-class housing in the Little Horton area. The club was effectively pushed up Great Horton Road by the urban sprawl that was driven by Bradford's industrial prosperity. In 1880 the cricket club, in conjunction with Bradford Rugby Club, secured a long lease on a piece of land that was to become Park Avenue. The rugby club, Yorkshire's oldest club formed in 1863, had been playing at Apperley Bridge. Initially a highly elitist club, but as winning the Yorkshire Cup became an important civic aim,

Bradford RFC evolved into a more democratic organisation in order to attract the best playing talent from across the town. Alongside the democratisation on the field, as the club became recognised as the town's sporting representative on a regional and increasingly national scale, it attracted a popular support that began to be counted in the thousands and later tens of thousands. The move to Park Avenue accelerated that process and spectator accommodation on the ground was regularly expanded during the 1890s and 1900s.

The development of Park Avenue saw the cricket ground used for county and touring matches – the Australians being early visitors. During the 1880s the rugby club was widely recognised as being the best club side in the country, supplying many internationals to the England first XV. Even after rugby's great split of 1895, when Bradford became founder members of what we know today as the Rugby League, the success continued justifying the club motto *nulli seconds*: second to none. However, by the early years of the 20th century Britain was rapidly nationalising. In sport nowhere was that more represented than the Football League. The election of Bradford City into the League in 1903 transformed the Valley Parade club into Bradford's civic representative on the sporting field. By contrast the once imperious Bradford Rugby Club felt trapped in the geographically constrained Rugby League, the subsequent loss of status keenly felt in the boardroom at Park Avenue. Thus in 1907 it was perhaps no surprise that, after a failed merger bid with Bradford City, the rugby club switched codes to become Bradford (Park Avenue) AFC.

Thus when the football ground was redeveloped by the renowned architect Archibald Leitch the architectural features used to adorn the stands were reflective of the history and self-image of the Bradford club and were arguably an attempt to restate the role of the Park Avenue club as the city's leading sporting organisation. The placing of the civic coat of arms on the main stand's gables and the lettering BFC (note Bradford Football Club as opposed to Bradford Park Avenue AFC) was highly symbolic. The new football club, backed by the enormous wealth of the club's benefactor and, in some people's eyes, autocrat Harry Briggs, Bradford (Park Avenue) was promoted to the first division within six years of gaining admission to the Football League. The 1914-15 season should have been the high water mark of Bradford's sporting history, with both Avenue and City in the top division. However, the outbreak of the Great War a few weeks before the start of the season completely overshadowed the remarkable rise of Bradford football which, as a professional sport, was a mere 11 years old.

Bradford's footballing prowess was illusory. The division of resources in a medium-sized city would prove fatal. The death of Harry Briggs in 1920 saw Avenue shorn of its main benefactor and by 1922 both Bradford clubs had been relegated from the top division. For the next 50 years both Bradford clubs were a source of great entertainment and pride to the people of the city. On every other winter Saturday at 3pm the referee's whistle would blow at Park Avenue while in the summer months Yorkshire County Cricket Club and Bradford League cricket offered long lazy days in the shadow of the magnificent pavilion. It would surely ever be thus? Sadly, over several decades Bradford's two professional football clubs effectively cancelled each other out. Additionally, the success of teams from neighbouring towns saw potential support leak out of the city. By the 1960s both clubs were encamped in the bottom two divisions and Avenue had to apply for re-election to the

Football League four times. In 1970 they failed and were replaced in the Football League by Cambridge United.

For three bleak seasons the club battled on in the Northern Premier League at Park Avenue. However, by 1973 an unpaid tax bill forced the sale of the famous ground. A 'farewell to Park Avenue' friendly was played against Bradford City in May 1973. It was a melancholy evening. The ground was already showing signs of dilapidation, with peeling paintwork and floodlights with half the bulbs blown. To add insult to injury City won by a solitary second half goal. At the final whistle the crowds walked away into the night for the final time, leaving 93 years of history in their wake.

Avenue soldiered on for one final season in exile at the Valley Parade home of their cross-town rivals Bradford City. With crowds declining it was decided to bow to the inevitable and in 1974 the club was wound up. At Park Avenue itself the football ground was abandoned to its fate. While plans for its reuse came and went, the grass on the field grew waist high and the weather and vandals began to take their toll on the stands. By 1980 the ground had deteriorated to such a dangerous state that the decision was taken to demolish the Main Stand and the roofs of the Horton End and Low Side. During the demolition process fans were allowed to enter the ground. Often a solitary supporter could be seen leaning on a crush barrier gazing into the middle distance, reviving cherished memories as slowly the old ground succumbed to the wrecker's ball. In 1986 Bradford Cricket Club abandoned their section of the ground and the beautiful pavilion shared the fate of its neighbouring football facilities, being vandalised to such an extent that demolition was an inevitability.

However, just as the ground appeared to have reached its nadir, green shoots began to appear and they were not confined to the saplings that were taking an ever greater hold on the terraces. Bradford Council returned the football field to a playable condition and local amateur football teams began to use the site. County cricket was enticed back to Park Avenue. However, part of the development included an indoor cricket facility that was constructed on the Canterbury Avenue end of the football ground which resulted in nearly half of the pitch being lost. Sadly, Yorkshire CCC played their last match on the ground in 1996. However, the former county ground remained in use being utilised by a vibrant local cricketing community.

In late 2015 plans were unveiled to undertake a major refurbishment of the cricket ground with a view to Yorkshire CCC returning in 2019. On the remainder of the football field 24 hour cricket nets are proposed to be erected. While this would turn the once multi-sport Park Avenue grounds into a single sport venue, at least it would ensure that sport would continue to be played and enjoyed at Park Avenue, as it has been for nearly 140 years.

Aerial photograph, probably 7 May 1966, when Bradford played Port Vale and lost 2-1 and Bradford CC played a Bradford League fixture against Lightcliffe

Yorkshire Cricketers' charity match, pictured in front of the Dolls House, 1946

8-2, 8-2. We beat Man City 8-2. Back in 1946, when we showed some tricks, and we beat Man City 8-2. Have You?
terrace chant

Talking about the Horton Park end terrace.

Graham: 'Our first date together, 1963 I think it was the start of the season. The first date was here, just to the left of the goal.'

Angela: 'I remember we picked up your Uncle Jim on the way.'

Graham: 'I first came in 1950. We came by train from Clayton. That was a lovely little trip on the train – it took five to ten minutes and we got off at Horton Park, right opposite the ground.'

Graham and Angela Firth

The vast majority of the trees on the terrace are self-seeded. Nature always finds a way of re-colonising civilization. But the vast majority of seeds would have come from the park at the Horton Park End. When our Victorian forefathers decided it was good for working people to have a bit of park, they were mostly planted with ornamental trees. But an awful lot of the trees such as Ash and Sycamore were planted because of their pollution benefits. Everyone had coal fires then and these trees were planted because they could absorb the pollution in the air.

It was amazing to see how nature had once more colonised, but it was also amazing to see how intact all the terraces were. I would like to see the whole terrace completely cleared.

Paul Waterhouse – landscape gardener and nurseryman

→
Tree: Ash
Scientific name: *Fraxinus excelsior*
Alan Ward
Photograph, 2015

'I am probably one of the younger fans in our gang that go home and away. But what we decided to do was make as much noise as possible and bring a lot of colour to grounds. So we bring a lot of flags. The club has a proud history and we are quite keen that even the younger fans know about it. We have modern and historic flags from the old Bradford Park Avenue ground.'

Lewis Sale

My initial interest in the project was twofold. I'm very interested in trees and had started a tree sketchbook just before you got in touch. I'd also been reading Richard Mabey who argues that neglected urban sites that are recolonised by nature play a vital role in wildlife conservation and that, despite their often unlovely appearance, they are ecologically very significant. BPA offered an excellent opportunity to continue working with trees and to record a self-seeded wood that has established itself on a derelict urban site with no human interference.

When I arrived my first interest was in the different tree species that have established themselves on the site. My first walks were slow and meandering around the site observing all the species I saw. This wasn't a 'proper' botanical survey and I'm not a trained botanist. But it was a careful observation by a well informed amateur and that's reasonable artistic field work! Over the three days I noted down 11 different species. It seemed like a very apt number – a species for each player in the team.

Next I looked at the relative numbers of different species. There are two predominant species – Ash and Sycamore (both large trees) – with an understory of smaller species in regular but fewer numbers (Hazel, Goat Willow, Elder). Also in the understory, but in much smaller numbers, were Hawthorn, Swedish Whitebeam and Rowan. In very small numbers I found Field Maple, Norway Maple and (I think) Caucasian Elm. Is there such a thing as 2 - 3 - 3 - 3 football formation?

Sketchbook spreads: Louise O'Reilly, botanical artist

Historic Bradford Park Avenue flag that originally flew over the ground

November 2013: clearing the leaves from the Horton Park End terrace
Overlay: detail from Bradford Park Avenue model by John Sucksmith

Donald Bell was the country's first professional footballer to enlist in the Great War and remains the only one ever to be awarded the Victoria Cross, which recognised his exceptional valour during service in the trenches in northern France on 5th July 1916. Just five days later, without even knowing he was to receive the nation's highest military honour, he was fatally shot in the head during a similar attack that saved the day for his comrades.

Full-back Bell played with Bradford Park Avenue from 1912 until November 1914 when he enlisted with the 9th Battalion of the Yorkshire Regiment (The Green Howards) and went to serve on the front line in the Battle of the Somme. He had previously played as an amateur with Newcastle United and Crystal Palace, as well as donning the jersey for a string of smaller clubs in earlier years.

E1323.2 Victoria Cross medal awarded to Donald Bell
Courtesy National Football Mueseum and Professional Footballers' Association

November 2013: archaeological dig and fans

→
14 Plastic Cups
Neville Gabie
Photograph, 2013

The scarf* belonged to my father Fred Denison. His first game was 27th December 1943, kick-off 3pm when Avenue entertained Leeds United in front of a crowd of 13,500 and beat them 2-1. They had some fantastic players at that time. Players like Len Shackleton, my father's favourite.

I cannot remember my first game but it would have been in the early 1960s. One of my heroes was Kevin Hector. I was at that famous game when he scored five goals when Avenue beat Barnsley 7-2. The goal I do remember though from that day was by Bobby Ham, which hit the crossbar and came back, hit the goalkeeper on the back and rebounded into the net. It is things like that you don't forget.

Keith Denison   * Scarf p. 7

→
Tree: Hazel
Scientific name: *Corylus avellana*
Alan Ward
Photograph, 2015

ASH. Common Ash, European Ash — Fraxinus excelsior

Compound: consisting of several leaflets joining a single leaf stalk (PETIOLE)

Pinnate: leaflets occur in pairs

Opposite: leaflets opposite pairs
 Single leaflet at top of leaf

Leaf margin serrated

Leaflet shape Eliptical (?)
 oval with long tips

3rd most common tree in Britain

Pointed, delicate, smooth

3.59pm, 14th November 2013: 1966 Penny, the first coin to be excavated during the dig at Bradford Park Avenue (c017)

Imagine 1966

England win the World Cup.

Kevin Hector received a gold watch from Bradford Park Avenue in recognition of his 45 goals for them during the 1965-66 season, and soon afterwards was sold to Derby County for a club record fee.

←

'Imagine 1966'
**Neville Gabie
Photograph, 2013**

October 1966

Sun 23 — Went out with Meagan (Plebs) went on scooter.

Mon 24 — Went to Meagan's house for evening after going to see her at 4-15. Really love her. Went on scooter

Tues 25 — Went to Meagan's house at 9-15 p.m. after watching Avenue lose to Derby 1-0. She says she will write to Mr. Ainsworth addressed to Meagan

Wed 26 — Meagan goes to Blackpool

Thur 27 — Wrote letter to Megan

Fri 28 — Received letter from Megan. Went to Barbeque at night got home 1-15

Sat 29 — v Luton A. DRAW 2-2 HAM, DEAKIN | Mother gave up left home 12-30

Oct/Nov 1966

Sun 30 — Meagan comes back from Blackpool. Went to her house at 5 in John's car. Went to pictures then back to her house on scooter

Mon 31 —

Tues 1 —

Wed 2 — Met Megan in BFD 7-45 went to Odeon then ran her home on scooter

Thur 3 — Went to Megan's house for evening. N.B. Bonfires

Fri 4 — Went to Megan's house on Dave's scooter then went to Heart Beth then back to her house

Sat 5 — v Bradford (Pk) A. WON 2-0 HAM, POTTS. Went with Megan to Cow & Calf by bus missed last bus. Went to Otley then to my house eventually

Down comes the snow—and up goes the ball. tipped over the bar by Bradford goalkeeper Hardie from a shot by Brighton centre forward Smith

Jason Wood

GOAL-LINE ARCHAEOLOGY

Goal-line technology supplies indisputable results in seconds; goal-line archaeology takes a little longer and provides ample cause for much head-scratching…

Topophilia – the emotional and subjective attachment to cherished places through the shared enjoyment of memory, nostalgia and the power of association.

Football and archaeology

Field archaeology is an essentially English form of sport   O.G.S. Crawford (1953)

Football and archaeology. Two words rarely seen in the same sentence; two subjects rarely thought of together. While football and archaeology may not be the most obvious or closest of bedfellows, this aspect of the project started from the premise that football, as an industry, must have by definition an industrial archaeology.

But before describing the discoveries, the concept of an 'archaeology of football' requires some introductory and contextual discussion. The heritage of sport is only one dimension of the historic environment but, in the case of football, it is a keenly distinctive aspect of place, memory and meaning. Research has shown that football grounds are valued as embodiments of history and repositories of public memory, with the power to stir hearts and minds and evoke strong visual, sensory and social responses. This is especially true when grounds are redeveloped or relocated as many have been in the UK since the 1990s. Cultural geographers have a word for this – topophilia; the emotional and subjective attachment to cherished places through the shared enjoyment of memory, nostalgia and the power of association. Topophilia is especially acute in relation to football grounds which convey an intense sense of identity and belonging. Sometimes, as in the case of Park Avenue, long after the venue itself has passed out of use or existence.

From football ground to tree-clad ruin

Football in the 1990s – the terraces disappeared but the fans did not.
At Park Avenue in the 1970s it was the fans that disappeared but the terraces remained.

Park Avenue was abandoned to a slow lingering death in 1973. It was partly demolished in 1980 since when it has been reclaimed by nature. The Kop or Horton Park End has vanished beneath a canopy of trees to such an extent that Google Maps records the site as an area of woodland. The crumbling, overgrown remains now more resemble an ancient ruin than a football ground. Park Avenue is the Angkor Wat of football.

Opportunities to dig at former football grounds are rare because of the problem of availability. Historic grounds have been either remodelled and are still in use or they have been demolished and redeveloped. Park Avenue was one of the first historic grounds to be abandoned but it survived redevelopment because of a restrictive covenant which only permits the site to be used for sport or recreation. It therefore escaped burial under a housing estate, supermarket or retail park and is accessible for excavation.

November 2013

Leaves from the forest of trees that now occupy the terraces at the Horton Park End were turning from green to autumnal red and amber, imitating the periodic changing of the club's colours. A great number had fallen over the former goal area. The first job was to sweep them up, producing the first find of the dig – a Styrofoam fast food carton.

Locating the exact position of the goal, and therefore where to dig to find one of the goalposts, was easier said than done. Demolition of Leitch's main stand and burial and partial re-landscaping of the touchline in front of it meant that the full width of the original pitch was no longer discernible. It was not going to be simply a case of measuring the width and dividing the figure in half to pinpoint the centre of the goal. The concrete perimeter wall curved at each corner and there were just enough of the beginnings of a curve at the corner with the main stand to estimate the width. There were also traces of the cinder track running in front of the perimeter wall to estimate its width, the likely depth of the goal and therefore the position of the goal-line.

Or so we thought …

With the leaves swept away, it was possible to detect a slight rise in the ground surface a little further south (towards the site of the main stand) from where our measurements had indicated. Perhaps this corresponded to the goal mouth area which often required re-turfing? This idea was soon confirmed when, prompted by a blurred photograph in an old newspaper cutting shown to us by a visitor, we took a more careful look at the perimeter wall. It now became clear that the otherwise white painted wall had once been painted red in the area behind and to the sides of the goal (in all likelihood to help differentiate the white goal net from the wall behind). This clinched it. The centre of the red painted area gave us the centre of the goal. The newspaper photograph, and other images, also suggested the cinder track was wider and the goal net deeper, so we revised our thinking on that score too – and started digging.

Left-hand goalpost

Having de-turfed and trowelled clean the subsoil over a 1.5m-wide trench between the goal-line and the perimeter wall, the position of the left-hand goalpost hole soon revealed itself. The hole was filled with much the same loamy soil as the turf layer but the soil was less compact and less gritty than the surface into which it was cut. As the excavation proceeded, the fill became loose and voids began to appear, exposing the top of something circular and white – perhaps the goalpost itself? Unlikely as the hole was clearly square, and anyway round or spherical posts were only introduced relatively recently. What could it be?

Unexpectedly, and with much hilarity, a stack of 14 plastic tea cups emerged, apparently deliberately deposited to mark the place of the goalpost. A discovery of this kind would not be out of place in a ritual context on a prehistoric site but to find this type of 'special deposit' replicated in a late 20th-century environment supplies an unusual illustration of topophiliac mentality.

Peter Barker beside the left-hand goalpost at the Horton Park End
after the final match played at Park Avenue

Horton Park End goal
detail from Park Avenue model by John Sucksmith

Jason Wood

April 2015

Before any further digging, it was decided to undertake some geophysical survey over the site of the main stand and also the pitch. The survey produced some remarkable results. Chris Gaffney, Head of School of Archaeological Sciences at the University of Bradford, takes up the story.

One of the misconceptions of my profession is that the public thinks that we use x-rays to detect the remnants of human occupation beneath the ground. In reality we use many different techniques, but none of them involve x-rays! When I was first asked about surveying at BPA the challenge was which, if any, technique we would use to find any 'archaeological' remains. Apart from maybe land drains, there are no structural remains or features cut into the ground at BPA that would resemble a traditional archaeological site. However, back in the first series of 'Time Team' I surveyed over a Roman road at Ribchester. Much to our surprise we found that earth resistance data detected not only the road but a ghostly image of a former football pitch. The low resistance image was probably due to structural changes in the soil resulting from liming of the pitch. I wondered if we could be lucky enough to see the same process at work at BPA?

Armed with our resistance meter we set off to train some students at BPA. The ground was beautifully level and the grass mown short; ideal for a good game of football and just as good for survey. As you can see from the results we did map some drains but significantly some of the pitch markings – the centre circle, halfway line and, at the Horton Park End, the penalty area and the six-yard box. Within the data you can see other trends that appear to be linked to heavy use of particular parts of the pitch.

The penalty area and the touchline nearest to the main stand dug-outs all show elevated levels of resistance and this is likely to reflect compression of the earth/re-seeding of damaged grass. If you were to excavate the pitch markings shown in our data, what are you likely you find? Apart from some slight texture changes in the topsoil, it is probable that these 'features' are invisible. I guess that the digital data that forms the image is the clearest view we will now get of the pitch at BPA.

Chris Gaffney

A student training day in April 2015 was followed by further surveys and demonstrations in September during the Bradford Science Festival.

September 2015

Trench 1

We did not require geophysics to locate the right-hand goalpost. Having found one it was easy, by measuring the regulation eight yards (or 7.315m), to find the other, and then to mark out the immediate playing area – six-yard box, penalty area and penalty spot, etc.

Our plan was to excavate the whole of the site of the goal to recover any evidence for how the goalposts and net were secured and to test the theory concerning re-turfing of the goal mouth area. But first we had to examine the deposits connected with the post-1973 use of the ground and its eventual demolition in 1980.

Below the turf, the subsoil was littered with fragments of the asbestos roof that originally covered the Horton Park End. Spread across the area were many of the metal hook bolts for fixing the corrugated sheets to the roof purlins, along with their associated hexagonal nuts and sealing washers. There were also numerous fragments of iron guttering. The chance find of a plastic roundel bearing the words 'New Duranite' initially confused us into thinking we might have identified the roofing contractor but on further investigation New Duranite proved to be the manufacturer's name for a water cistern, so it probably came from the toilet block at the back of the terrace.

Moving the goalposts? What appeared to be a non-regulation goalpost hole, lying between the original ones and slightly forward of the goal-line, may have related to the reduced-size pitch used by Sunday League footballers post 1973. The hole was packed with stone, brick and gutter fragments reused from the roof destruction. Other finds probably relating to this period included plastic football boot studs, tin cans, bottle tops, glass bottle fragments, plastic pen tops, a plastic knife and fork and a number of small denomination early decimal coins.

Once these later levels had been removed it was possible to understand the layout of the whole goal area and to locate and excavate the right-hand goalpost hole. Unsurprisingly, this proved to be identical in shape and size to the left-hand goalpost hole (square, 20cm x 18cm) but did not contain any plastic tea cups. The fill did contain part of the brick lining that had broken and collapsed, presumably when the post was extracted. The brick was made at Birkby's, a local brickworks in Wyke.

When we first started to encounter one or two of the roof hook bolts in November 2013, we were fooled into thinking they might have been hooks to hold the goal net fast in the ground or to attach it to the posts. The sheer number of these hooks encountered in 2015, however, soon put an end to that theory. Distinguishing between roof hooks and net hooks became a bit of a challenge, especially as many had rusted beyond easy recognition. A number of hooks could be clearly identified as holding the net in the ground as they were still upright in the earth. Others, too narrow to be roof fixings, lay scattered behind or to the side of the goal. These were assumed to be net hooks. There were also several smaller hooks which undoubtedly held the net to the posts.

Excavation went deeper in the 1.5m strip originally excavated in 2013. Here, the area around and behind the left-hand goalpost hole was found to be a hard packed surface of clay and clinker mixed with some stones. This seems to have been placed there to provide a stronger anchor point for the ground hooks.

The laws of the game decree that the crossbar has to be horizontal and that the distance from

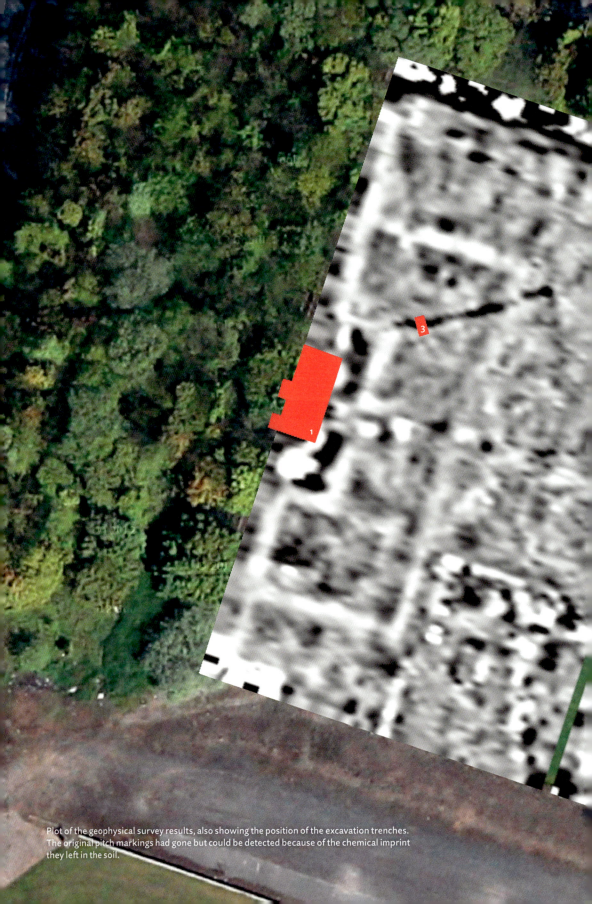

Plot of the geophysical survey results, also showing the position of the excavation trenches. The original pitch markings had gone but could be detected because of the chemical imprint they left in the soil.

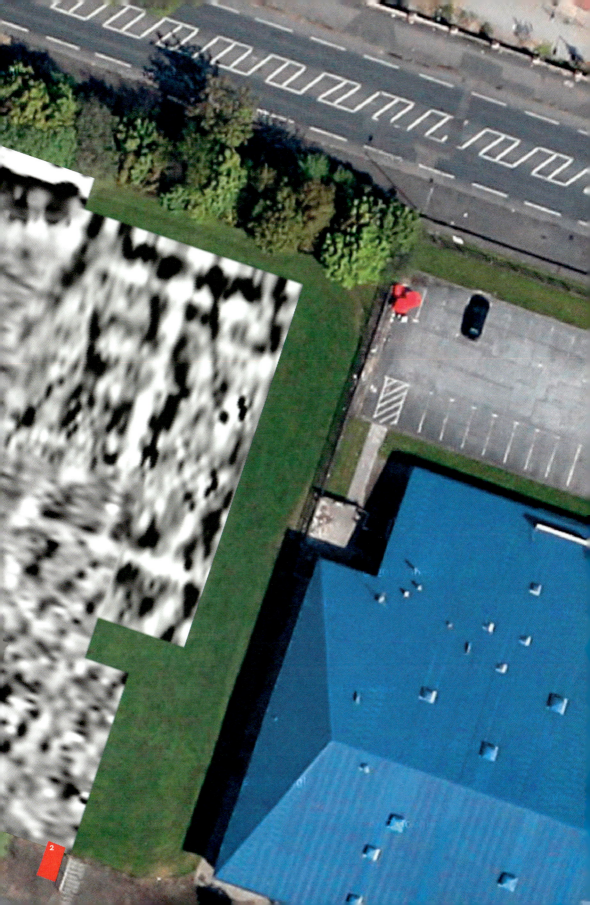

Brick made at Henry Birkby & Sons Ltd, Storr Hill Brickworks, Wyke, Bradford (right-hand goalpost hole)

New Duranite roundel (OTH010)

Gutter fragments (FE017)

Hook bolts (FE033, FE057, FE081),
hexagonal nuts (FE032, FE038) and washer (FE031)

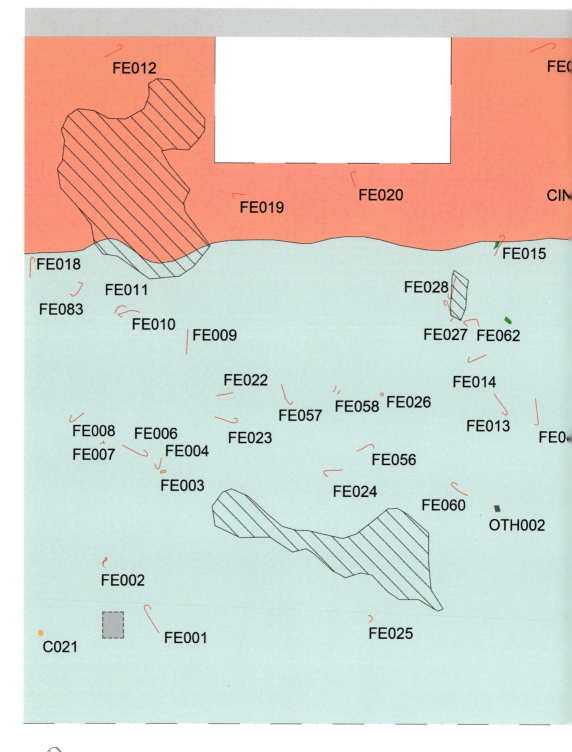

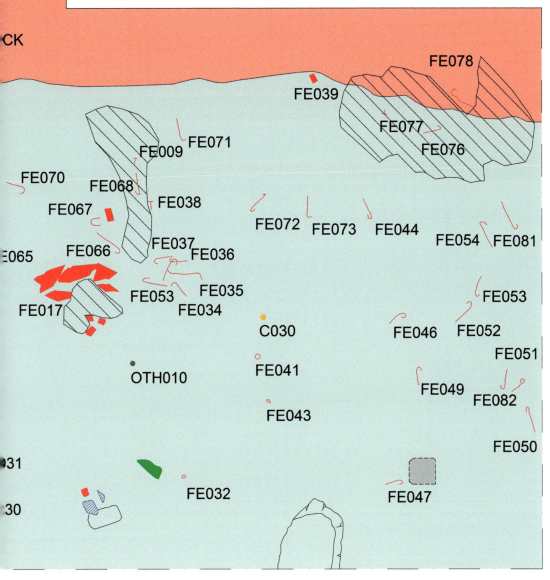

the lower edge of the crossbar to the ground should be eight feet (2.44m). But what happens when the pitch between the touchlines is on a slope, as is the case at Park Avenue? Was the fact that the right-hand goalpost hole was not as deep as that on the left significant in this regard? Was the differential deliberate to compensate for the slope? It seemed unlikely as the law says the crossbar has to be horizontal. But if the ground slopes and the crossbar is horizontal, then the distance between the crossbar and the ground would not be the regulation eight feet. This led to some perplexing discussion and caused us to look again at the goalmouth area rather than trying to imagine various scenarios where the goal frame became more and more distorted. (Neville had published hundreds of photographs of goalposts around the world, many fabulously distorted, and so was particularly vocal on the subject.) Having marked out the six-yard box it became clear that the goal mouth was in fact level, even though the rest of the penalty area sloped. The box had been purposely terraced into the slope to provide a flat surface in front of the goal, enabling the crossbar to be horizontal and consistently eight feet above the ground. The different depths of the goalpost holes had been a red herring.

As well as being level, the area between the goalposts and into the six-yard box was gritty and compact. This layer, seen in section in the sides of the goalpost holes, was about 10cm deep. The base of the layer is thought to represent the original pitch level of 1907, and the layer itself the subsequent build up of the ground due to re-seeding or re-turfing throughout the pitch's lifetime through to 1973. Paul Waterhouse, a landscape gardener and nurseryman who helped out on the dig, advised us that the grittiness was due to top dressing with sharp sand when re-seeding. If re-turfing was required then the preference was always for Northumberland turf (as used at the old Wembley) as it was known to be hard wearing. The supplier may have been the Sports Turf Research Institute in nearby Bingley.

As a regular part of the ground maintenance, it would have been necessary to spike the goal mouth to allow drainage and aeration of the soil. That the area was relatively well drained was confirmed by the discovery of a land drain running in front of the goal-line (the drain also shows on the geophysical survey). Part of the drain had collapsed causing the earth above to slump and become filled with destruction debris.

So our objectives had been met. We had found evidence for how the goalposts and net had been secured and confirmed ideas about re-turfing and levelling of the goal mouth area. What else might we expect to find? A football boot stud maybe (we found four); also two fragments of a pink plastic comb and the arm from a broken pair of spectacles – we joked that these items belonged to the goalie. What we were not expecting was the discovery of 55 coins, six marbles and a nappy pin. Thanks to the stories and memories shared by the large number of fans who came to visit us, the reason why we found these objects became apparent.

The pre-decimal coins were scattered over the footprint of the goal. They were small denomination (35 pennies, 17 halfpennies and 3 threepenny bits) ranging in date from 1900 to 1967. Appropriately, the first coin to be found was minted in 1966. Coincidently, there was also a 1907 halfpenny – minted the same year the football ground was built. Coins are usually a godsend for an archaeologist in helping to date layers or features, but in this instance of course the dates of the coins bore no significance as all would have been legal tender over the lifetime of the ground's use.

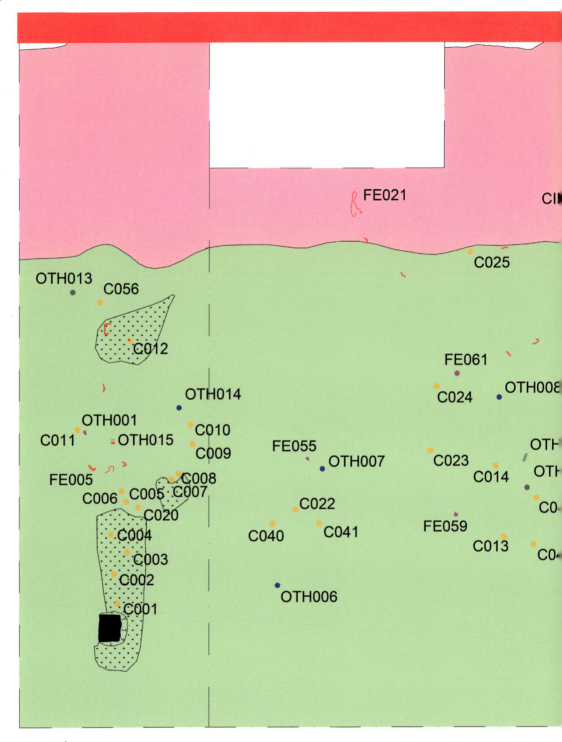 HARD-PACKED CLAY AND CLINKER   GROUND HOOK IN SITU

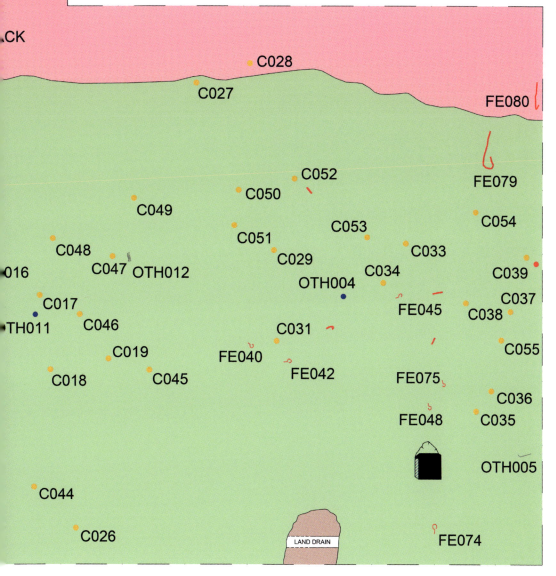

November 2013: Measuring and recording the left-hand goalpost and finds
It was brick lined to provide support and still contained some fragments of wood at the base, probably the remains of chocks used to brace the post

Jason Wood, archaeologist

Ground hooks (FE021, FE079, FE080)

Post hooks (FE005, FE040, FE042, FE045, FE048, FE074, FE075)

Football boot studs (OTH001, FE055, FE059, FE061)

Marbles (OTH0004, OTH006, OTH007, OTH008, OTH011, OTH014)

The pressing question was what were they doing there? Inevitably there were half-joking references to coins thrown at the goalie. But there were far too many (unless he was a really bad keeper) and anyway the offence of throwing coins at players is a relatively recent trend. There had to be another reason.

The answer came from an elderly fan, confirmed later by others. At half time, the club permitted collections for local charities and good causes – towards the end the good cause was the survival of the club! Apparently this involved four youths parading around the cinder track holding the corners of a large sheet, encouraging fans on the terraces to throw coins and then catching them in the sheet. The coins we found obviously missed their target, either hitting the net or going through it where they presumably were not easily retrieved. There was a concentration of coins behind the left-hand goalpost where they had hit the side-netting and fallen in a line. The position of these coins, along with the ground hooks, provided further evidence for the depth of the goal.

The marbles, we can now confirm, *were* thrown at the goalie. The culprit identified himself to us and sheepishly owned up to his youthful misdemeanour, which at the time got him evicted from the ground.

The last totally unexpected find, and the most bizarre, was a nappy pin. Unearthed next to one of the ground hooks behind the left-hand goalpost, the pin's presence in this context would have taken some explaining were it not for the fortuitous arrival a hour or so before the discovery of Susan Farr, daughter of Chick Farr, a former Bradford goalkeeper.

Polaroid spectacles (OTH005)

Pink comb (OTH003, OTH012)

Jason Wood

Trench 2

A trial trench was opened into the re-landscaped slope covering the touchline in front of Leitch's main stand with the intention of digging out a dug-out, or rather finding a dug-out to dig. Opinions seemed to differ as to the location of the dug-outs. Photographic evidence was inconclusive but suggested the two dug-outs were not equidistant from centre line. Geophysics was unlikely to help because of the slope. Oral evidence was weak but older fans recalled seeing benches between the touchline and the perimeter wall, rather than dug-outs. The consensus was that the dug-outs were added to the rear face of the perimeter wall (so not dug-outs as such) and probably after substitutes were allowed from the start of the 1965-66 season.

Marking out trench 2, location of the Archibald Leitch Stand. and its excavation, 2015

Due to the limited size of the trench and the anticipated overburden resulting from demolishing the main stand in 1980, it soon became evident that we would do well to find the perimeter wall, never mind a dug-out. In the event the wall and even the cinder track eluded us and we contented ourselves with locating the edge of the pitch and hacking our way through over a metre of destruction debris and rubble, before calling it a day. Finds included elements of the roof (wood, slate and lead), York stone flags thought to have come from the floor of the bar in this area, and other objects perhaps associated with the bar and its clientele (glass bottles, various ceramics, metals and plastics, a Golden Wonder crisp packet, clay pipe stem, pair of scissors, drawer handle, a few pre-decimal and early decimal coins, a copper bracelet and lady's shoe. Sounds like quite a party.

Trench 3

The geophysics detected what appeared to be a number of parallel land drains under certain areas of the pitch, particularly running across the half-way line. One very clear example lay on a diagonal within the right-hand edge of the penalty area, probably joining the aforementioned drain excavated in front of the goal-line. Drains like these were laid to deal with particular problem areas, such as the presence of a natural spring, rather than necessarily over the entire pitch. They were relatively expensive so not usually laid where they were not required.

We excavated a small sondage to test the drain theory and found what we were looking for – a drain, about 50-60cm deep, its base lying on a bed of ash and clinker above the natural clay.

Some 90th-minute thoughts

The attraction of witnessing and participating in an archaeological dig evidently caught the imagination of the many fans, local residents and school children who visited the site (including the club mascot). The excavation was relatively small but because it focused on a familiar and readily imaginable part of the ground – the goal area – and because the goalpost holes and ground hooks were clearly visible in the earth, the discoveries generated extraordinary interest, even among those too young to have known the ground in its heyday.

There is an attraction too for archaeologists of the recent past who work on sites such as Park Avenue. Archaeologists specialising in more distant times simply cannot benefit from guys showing up with 40-year-old photographs of themselves standing next to the very thing you have just dug up. But there are also salutary lessons on the limitations of archaeology as a stand alone methodology. Clearly certain archaeological methodologies can aid our understanding of football history but one might also ask how football history might aid our understanding of the material culture revealed by archaeology. And can an archaeology of football help us explore and better understand wider archaeological questions and theories? How, for instance, would it have been remotely possible to interpret the presence of over 50 coins and a nappy pin without the relevant oral testimonies? Yet these stories would have remained untold if it was not for the Breaking Ground project and the material culture that prompted the questions in the first place.

Trench 3, pitch drainage pipes, 2015

School visit and club mascot during excavation of the goal mouth area, Horton Park End, 2015

September 2015: goalmouth dig and equipment

Open day tour by David Pendleton for fans and members of public

Whilst on the excavation, it turned out that I had a personal history with the football ground.

My Grandfather had once tried to join the team. When it came to the first day of training, he had been fed a large dinner, which subsequently made its reappearance during training.

It was a great pleasure to work on the dig, to hear the personal histories from the supporters, to excavate such a historic ground which helped found the city's football past. I feel extremely grateful to have had the chance to work on such a site which not only had a local living past that remembered the grounds and the games, but also to have had a personal link to it as well.

My father told me that I was born on 11th July 1950 and I saw my first game in August 1950. So I obviously don't remember it.

Peter Barker

→
Tree: Hazel (?)
Scientific name: *Corylus avellana*
Alan Ward
Photograph, 2015

Food plant for caterpillars of sycamore moth, plumed prominent + maple prominent

leaves
palmate
5 lobes

flat
mid-green

Native to central, eastern & Southern Europe
Introduced into UK in Middle ages (1403)

SYCAMORE

Acer pseudoplatanus
Maple "like a plane tree"

red petiole

FOOTBALL LEAGUE – FOURTH DIVISION
BRADFORD V SCUNTHORPE UNITED
SATURDAY, 4TH APRIL, 1970, KICK-OFF 3.00PM

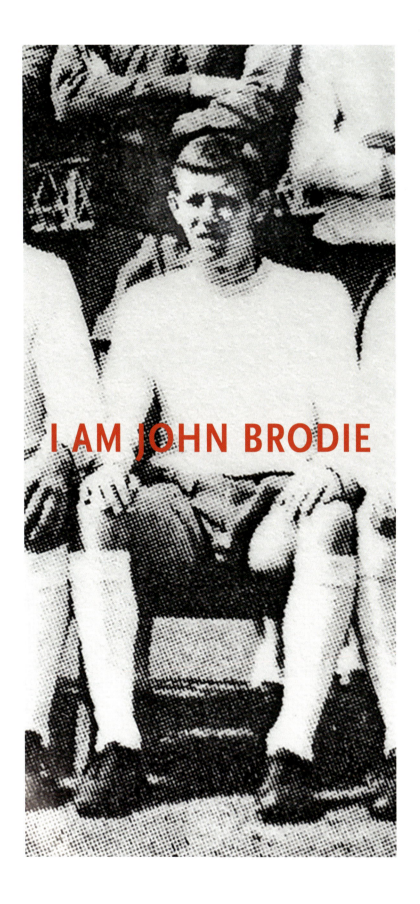

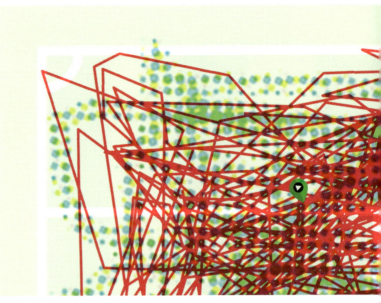

SATURDAY, 12TH SEPTEMBER 2015, KICK-OFF 3.00PM: ALAN WARD ADOPTED THE PERSONA OF JOHN BRODIE AND RE-IMA

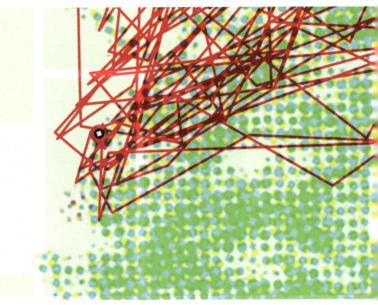

Bradford: Hickman, Dolan, Brodie, Atkinson, Campell, Carr, Woolmer, Tewey, Charnley, Brannan, Thom. Sub Wright
Scunthorpe: Barnard, Foxton, Jackson, Linday, Deere, Welbourne, Keegan, Cassidy, Kerr, Heath, Davidson. Sub Atkin
Referee: Mr D. Pugh (Chester) **Attendance:** 2563

The small crowd were urging on the Avenue players, but it was Scunthorpe who went ahead in the 17th minute. KERR was the scorer. Cassidy beat the Avenue defence with ease, and Kerr ran on to beat Hickman to the ball.
[Stanley Pearson, Telegraph and Argus, Football Pink]

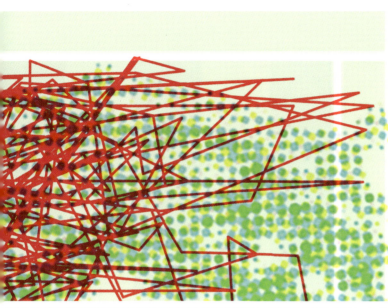

RST FORTY-FIVE MINUTES PLAYED DEFENDING THE HORTON PARK END GOAL AGAINST SCUNTHORPE & KEVIN KEEGAN

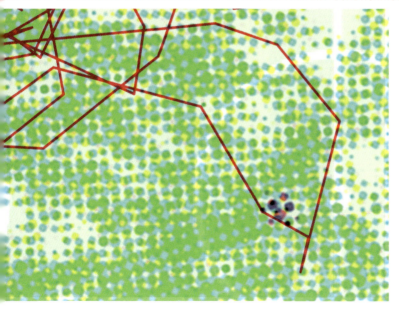

SAM DOLLMAN, ARCHAEOLOGY STUDENT
ALAN TEWLEY

DATE: 11TH SEPTEMBER 2015, 3.17PM

KERR, SCUNTHORPE
DANIELLE FARRAR, ARCHAEOLOGY STUDENT

CHRIS GAFFNEY, ARCHAEOLOGICAL SCIENCES, UNIVERSITY OF BRADFORD
TONY WOOLMER

DAVID PENDLETON, SOCIAL HISTORIAN
CASSIDY(?) SCUNTHORPE

TREVOR ATKINSON
MICK PENDLETON,
VOLUNTEER ARCHAEOLOGIST

GEOFF HICKMAN
JASON WOOD, LEAD ARCHAEOLOGIST

DANIEL CAMPBELL
ROBERT NICHOLS,
ARCHAEOLOGIST

JOHN BRODIE TRANSFERRED TO PORT VALE THE FOLLOWING SEASON WHERE HE PLAYED FOR SIX YEARS. KNOWN FOR HARD TACKLING, HE MADE 179 APPEARANCES AND SCORED 2 GOALS. HE BROKE HIS LEG THREE TIMES.

KEVIN KEEGAN TRANSFERRED TO LIVERPOOL THE FOLLOWING SEASON, WHERE HE PLAYED FOR SIX YEARS. HE MADE 230 APPEARANCES AND SCORED 68 GOALS, BECOMING THE FIRST 'SUPERSTAR' ENGLISH PLAYER.

Is Chick Farr really your dad?

Much loved for his on the field antics and goalkeeping prowess, it is rumoured that during a match the elastic waistband of his shorts snapped and they fell to his ankles. The trainer rushed onto the pitch with an emergency safety pin to keep them up, to the hilarity of the fans on the terraces. For weeks after the incident Chick Farr received 'spare' nappy pins through the post, or had them thrown onto the pitch when he was in goal.

He kept them all in an old tobacco tin.

Chick Farr's daughter Susan was sitting on the perimeter wall telling this story when one of the archaeologists who had overheard the conversation brought over a rusted nappy pin, which had just been uncovered in the goalmouth.

COPYRIGHT. ALL RIGHTS RESERVED.
Tottenham Hotspur Football & Athletic Company, Limited.

Official Programme
And Record of the Club.

Issued every Match Day.   PRICE ONE PENNY.

Vol. XXXI. No. 20   NOVEMBER 12, 1938.

Crusha & Son, Ltd., Tottenham, Enfield, Palmers Green and Wood Green.

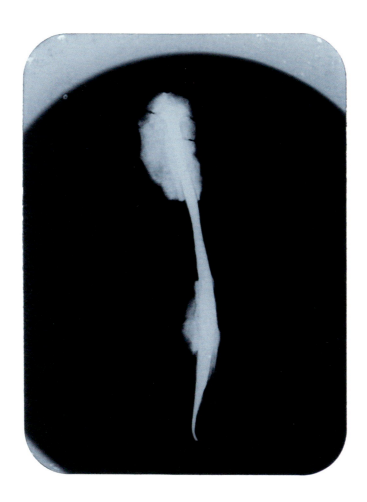

Nappy Pin
Neville Gabie
X-ray Photograph, 2015

Members of the
Football Association.

The Football League
(Third Division).

The West Riding County F.A.

The Midland Counties Football League.

The Yorkshire League.

The Northern Intermediate League.

'Phone Bradford 28000.

GROUND—
PARK AVENUE.

BRADFORD (PARK AVENUE)
ASSOCIATION FOOTBALL CLUB
LIMITED

CLUB COLOURS—
RED, AMBER AND BLACK

Champions
The Third Division (Northern Section) 1927-28.
Midland Combination 1927-28, 1928-29.
The Yorkshire League 1920-21, 1922-23, 1928-29.
Northern Mid-Week League 1928-29, 1929-30.
The Midland Counties Football League 1931-32.
Yorkshire Mid-Week League 1933-34, 1935-36.
Winners of the West Riding Senior Cup 1910-11, 1912-13, 1923-24, 1926-27, 1931-32, 1935-36, 1950-51, 1952-53.
Winners of the West Riding Supplementary Cup 1928-29.

S. WADDILOVE, Chairman.
G. H. BRIGG, Secretary.
N. KIRKMAN, Manager.

REGISTERED OFFICE :
PARK AVENUE,
BRADFORD.

28th July, 1953.

TO WHOM IT MAY CONCERN

  Mr. T. F. Farr was employed by this Club as a professional player from 29th September, 1934 to 31st July, 1950 and as an assistant trainer from 1st August, 1950 to 6th June, 1953. He ceased to be employed on the latter date consequent upon a decision of the Directors to curtail expenditure by reducing staff because of the Club's financial difficulties.

  As a player Mr. Farr rendered loyal and meritorious service whilst in his capacity as an assistant trainer he conscientiously and industriously carried out the duties assigned to him.

  We found him to be a man of excellent character, honest and sober in habits and one whose general conduct both on and off the field was at all times exemplary.

  Throughout his service here Mr. Farr has had the Club's interests at heart and I am certain that he will work for any other employer with the same zeal and faithfulness as he did for us.

Geo. H. Brigg
Secretary.

Eddie Parris made his debut in January 1929, scoring his team's only goal in a drawn F.A. Cup match against Hull, and thereafter established a regular first-team place at left wing. In his career at Bradford Park Avenue, he played 142 League and Cup games and scored 39 goals. In December 1931 Parris made his first and only appearance for Wales against Ireland in Belfast, becoming the first black player to represent Wales in an international.   Wikipedia

**The West Riding County Cup medal was brought to the open day
by his granddaughter Jan Richards, who still lives near the old ground**

Saturday, January 17th 1914. English League.
Leeds City, at Park Avenue.
Bradford 3 goals: Leeds City 1 goal.
Crabble: Watson. Blackham: Garry. Mavin. Scott:
Kivlichan. Little. Smith. Bauchop. McCandless.
Scorers: Smith (2) & Bauchop.

Saturday, January 24th. 1914. English League.
Clapton Orient, at Homerton.
Bradford 0 goals: Clapton 1 goal.
Crabble: Watson. Blackham: Garry. Mavin. Scott:
Kivlichan. Little. Smith. Bauchop. McCandless.

Saturday, January 31st. 1914. English Cup, 2nd Round.
Sheffield United, at Bramall Lane.
Bradford 1 goal: Sheffield United 3 goals.
Crabble: Watson. Blackham: Garry. Mavin. Scott.
Kivlichan. Little. Smith. Bauchop. Leavey.
Scorer: Smith.

Saturday, February 7th 1914. English League.
Glossop, at Park Avenue. Tommy Little's Benefit.
Bradford 2 goals: Glossop 1 goal.
Crabble: W. G. McConnell. Blackham: Garry. Mavin.
Scott: Kivlichan. Little. Smith. Bauchop. McCandless.
Scorers: Little & Smith.

←
Casts of the Horton Park End goalpost holes
Neville Gabie
Photographs, 2015

→
Tree: Ash
Scientific name: *Fraxinus excelsior*
Alan Ward
Photograph, 2015

April 2015

Common Ash
Fraxinus excelsior

Ash buds opening.
8 Acre Wood, Rendham

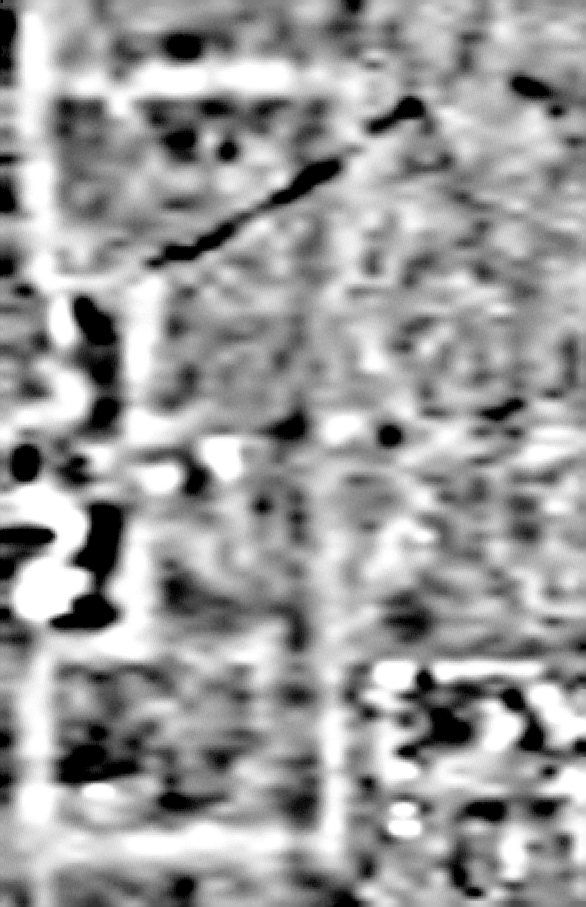

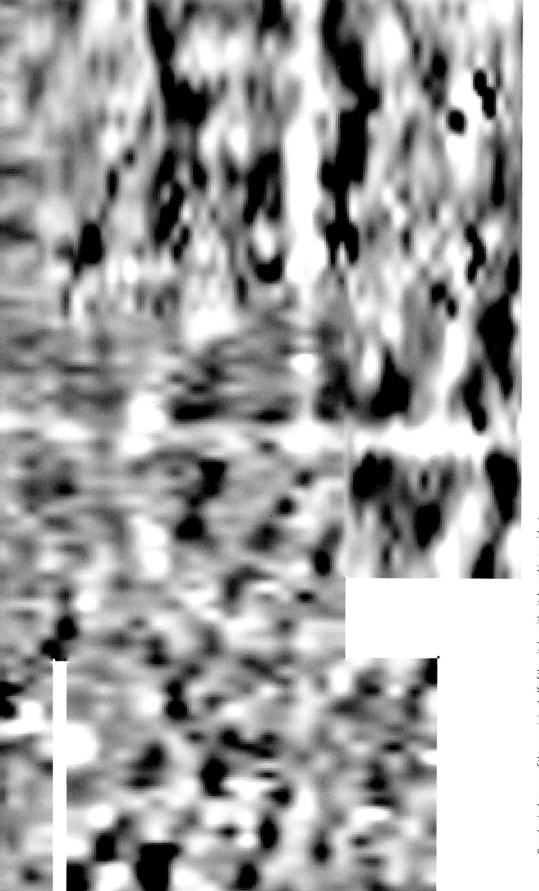

Geophysical survey of the remaining half of the pitch - with pitch markings evident

Geophysical Resistence Meter with pitch marked up in grid pattern
Survey by the School of Archaeological Sciences, University of Bradford

A vinyl record doesn't just reproduce sound: in its grooves it gives sound a physical texture – a warm texture that connoisseurs nostalgically claim the record transfers to the sounds it reproduces. Yet quite obviously the physical texture of the grooves and the sound they produce are in no way commensurate. Yet one would struggle to deny the quality conferred on the listening experience. In its new, temporal sound guise, the geophysical data whirrs and cracks in ways not drastically dissimilar to the whistles and rumblings that echo through the fissures and cracks in the football terrace.

The mapping of physical – yet unseen – space undertaken by the geophysical survey is transformed from a spatio-visual form of presentation (the digital image) in to a temporal-aural form of presentation (the modulation of sound over time). While our relation to the geophysical data itself has been de-spatialised (the data that was intended to be used to create an image of objects underground has now been transformed into sound data) its new temporal dimension allows us to experience the data in a much more visceral way.

Extracts from artists' notebooks: Oliver Palmer and Giorgio Garippa

Pitch
Oliver Palmer and Giorgio Garippa
Vinyl record
Duration: Approx. 40 mins
Edition: 50

Side A: Pitch
1: Pitch

Side B: Covenant
1 – 5: Pitch (Geophysical Survey data alternative takes and clips)
6 – 8: Gaps, Cracks and Fissures (recordings from the terrace)
9 – 11: Fan Interviews
12: Covenant

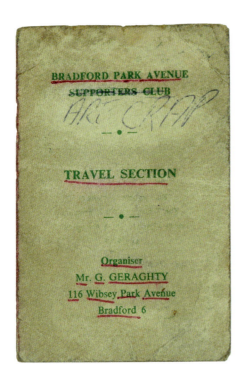

I first attended Park Avenue in 196
My father took me to the game wh
Jimmy Scoular made his debut as
player / manager. We played Alde
that day and won one nil and if
memory serves me correctly John
Buchanan scored the goal.

I remember particularly the old Pa
Avenue was just a magnificent pla
and over the years I had the pleas
watch some really good players.

I remember the 1961 season we go
promotion along with Peterborou
Crystal Palace and Northampton.
I remember the game with
Peterborough was postponed bu
the rearranged evening game had
attendance of over 20,000, which
quite a crowd.

Graham Lee

→
Tree: Sycamore
Scientific name: *Acer pseudoplatanus*
Alan Ward
Photograph, 2015

| | Common tree name: Ash
Scientific name: *Fraxinus excelsior* | | Common tree name: Hazel
Scientific name: *Corylus avellana* |

| | Common tree name: Sycamore
Scientific name: *Acer* | | Common tree name: Goat Willow
Scientific name: *Salix caprea* |

'Ash, Sycamore, Sycamore, Ash …'
Louise O'Reilly (in conjunction with Alan Ward)

BRADFORD (PARK AVENUE) F.C.
FROM LEFT: TREVOR PEEL., GEOFF GOULD, PHILIP ROBINSON, JO
PETER McBRIDE, KENNY HIBBITT, ALAN TURNER, PAUL I'A

Y, GEOFF LLOYD, IAN HUGHES, TREVOR BURGIN, JOHN HARDIE, LL BARNES, BOBBY HAM, GERARD LIGHTOWER.

Generally regarded as the greatest player ever to have worn an Avenue shirt is the late Len Shackleton, who started his Avenue career in the Wartime League programme in 1940, and who, up to his death, was a Vice President of the present club. "Shack" scored more goals for Avenue than any other player (171 in total) and was chosen for England in the victory international at Hampden Park in 1946.

The stuff of legend – after a 3–1 first leg defeat at home in front of 25,014 in the FA Cup, and a six goal drubbing by City just prior to that, Bradford travelled to Manchester for the second leg.

On his day Len Shackleton, 'the Clown Prince of Soccer' could be almost unplayable and the match at Maine Road on 30 January 1946 was to be one of those days.

Writing in his autobiography the future West Ham and England manager Ron Greenwood, signed from Chelsea at the end of the war, recalled "Our cause seemed hopeless and to rub things in our coach ran into a blizzard right on top of the Pennines on our way to Maine Road for the second leg. Len Shackleton said 'let's turn back ... we don't stand a chance anyway.'"

They arrived at the ground with less than 20 minutes to spare and a pitch covered with pools of water and a gale blowing. It was to be a famous day for the West Yorkshire side. Manchester City were literally blown away, beaten 8-2, with Jackie Gibbons, a former Spurs amateur centre-forward, scoring four times. Ron Greenwood said, 'The sight of the great Frank Swift picking the ball out of the net eight times is something I shall never forget. Everything went right for us. It was one of those days.'

Returning home Len Shackleton's dad consoled him when he reported the score was 8-2. He didn't believe his son when he said Avenue had won and it needed the sight of the score in the newspaper the following morning to convince him.

Club website and Mark Metcalf

It's a unique bottle, it's signed by the great man.
I keep it in the fridge to keep it in perfect condition.

Andrew Pinfield

Around 1900 a most peculiar incident occurred at the Horton stadium. The groundsman, a chap by the name of Jennings, noticed from his house that a bright light was shining from the pavilion. The sighting puzzled Mr Jennings, as he had been at the ground only an hour previously, so set out to investigate.

Jennings walked across the dark ground arriving at the pavilion, he was somewhat startled to see a player in full standing staring back at him. Mr Jennings called for a police officer and the pair returned to the locked pavilion to find no light and no sport player. It was reported that Jennings was stone cold sober. The Park Avenue ghost sighting was never explained.

From *Park Avenue of Remembrance*
Brian Jeeves

That place from nine until 14 was my kingdom. A sadness falls over me every time I drive Horton Park Avenue. Ghosts everywhere as I pass it today.

Mike Stead

1887-8 season ticket and Southampton Street, Bradford, 2016

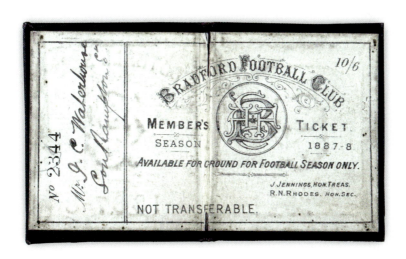

Signs from the former stadium, Tim Clapham

Fragments of the Bradford Park Avenue sign from above the main stand

Close-season, exhibition tennis match on the pitch, 1956

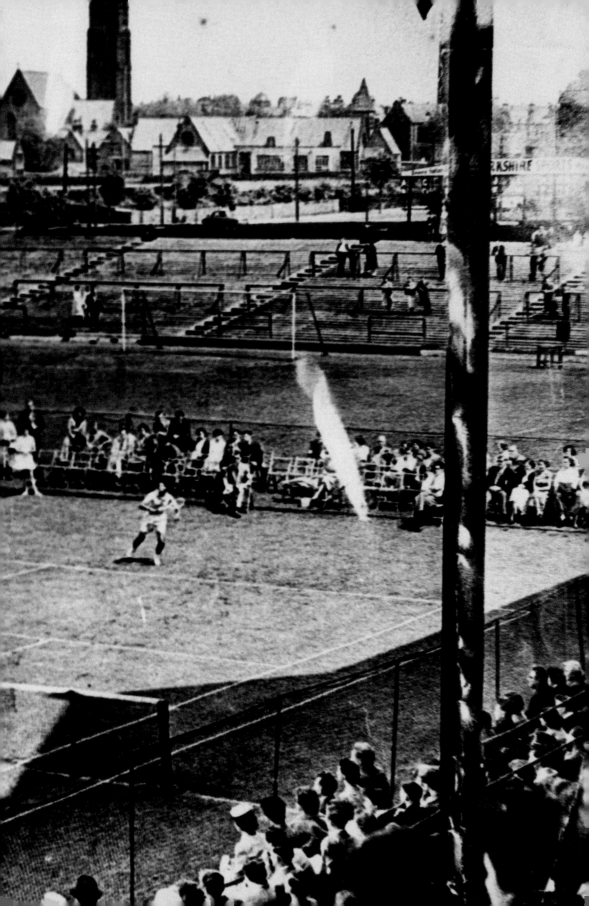

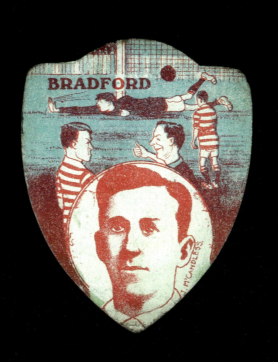

SPORT

Price: SIXPENCE

Vol. 4, No. 12 — INCORPORATING: "SPORT & AMUSEMENT GUIDE" — WEEKLY MAGAZINE — Mar. 20th, 1948

BRADFORD (P.A.) F.C.

Standing: Henry, White, Hepworth, Farr, Farrell, Downie.
Sitting: Smith, Ainsley, Greenwood, Elliott, Deplidge.

GRAND NATIONAL SUMMING-UP

I thought the only way I am going to get a proper perspective was to build a model.

It took a couple of years just to get everything together – any photographs I could find. I would go to the ground on a Saturday when they were playing cricket and wander around what was left of the terraces at the Horton Park End. I just started taking measurements; counting the number of steps on the terrace, seeing where the turnstiles used to be. Then just putting it together with all the photographs I had collected over the years. Although there are still some blind spots.

I started the model in August thinking it would be finished by Christmas, but it took another year, so 18 months altogether. I did the main stand first – the gable ends, because I thought if I cannot get this right there was no point in doing the rest of the ground. That took me three months – it took all of December just to do the roof.

It started off really as an art project but then I got really interested in the architecture and bought a book about Archibald Leitch. But it is also a time capsule and it allows people to go back. Like you say, it rekindles their memories

John Sucksmith

The photograph by John Sucksmith's father that inspired the model

HOME	VISITORS
CHANGES	

Football supporters either followed Bradford City or Bradford Park Avenue, but I remembered one little old man who use to stand on the half-way line wearing both a City and Avenue scarf. Supporters would also change ends at half-time. On Good Friday 1965 Avenue were playing away at Tranmere. My friend and I went on the supporters' bus from Park Avenue, she sat up to the early hours to finish knitting a green and white scarf. On the way back to the bus, after the match, a Tranmere supporter took the scarf from around her neck and ran off with it.

Susan Davies

We had a family tradition, we would always go shopping on a Saturday morning in Bradford town centre. One Saturday my mother said to me 'If you are a good lad your dad will take you to the football at Bradford Park Avenue this afternoon'. Sure enough he took me to the football match. At half time he gave me some money and sent me off to the club shop – he said 'You go buy something.' I must have been around ten or 11 – I am looking around this club shop at all the things and I saw this pennant in the top corner and it had a lovely trophy on it and I thought – alright I will buy that. So I bought the pennant and proudly took it to show my father. He just said 'What did you buy that for?' and I replied 'Because it has a lovely badge and trophy.' He said 'Yes but it says Manchester City on it.' I don't think that was what he was expecting.

Andrew Overby

Robert Nichols

PARK AVENUE WAS A PEOPLE'S PALACE

I am ashamed to admit I didn't know a great deal about Bradford Park Avenue before 2015 except that it is a name forever steeped in football folklore. They were a club that went out of the league and out of existence when that sort of thing wasn't really supposed to happen but against all the odds the name, the legend and amazingly the ground all lived on.

The one thing I do know all about is that former grounds still have a life after the last football has been kicked. People remain emotionally attached. Personally I couldn't stand to leave my beloved Ayresome Park, the home of Middlesbrough FC for nearly a century, and so bought a house on the site. Today I see myself as one of the guardians to the secrets of the site. I often give people tours following the sculpture trail as laid out by lead artist on the Bradford Park Avenue project, Neville Gabie.

Despite it being 20 years ago now since the stands and pitch were replaced by a housing estate the lure of the former ground continues. It might seem unlikely but something of the atmosphere seems to somehow remain locked in the stories that surround the sculptures that mark out parts of the pitch. This is precious heritage. It is a piece of sporting, social history, a temple where we worshipped and it still acts as a real draw for the community.

Bradford Park Avenue's old ground is all the more fascinating, a fossilised ground that has incredibly, incredulously survived in the middle of the city. Almost like the stumps of an ancient petrified forest surfacing from the seabed at low tide the foundations of a football ground have fought to remain, even against invasions of nature and man made structures. The masonry of the outer walls still stand tall and proud and there remain even the recesses for the turnstiles with the price chalked up in old money, 5 shillings. Clear back the encroaching woodland and the concrete steps of the Kop end spring forth again. I posted photographs on Facebook and received likes from all over the country, people were spell bound by this amazing place.

We went further in the project and peeled back the topsoil and turf and immediately among the debris of the old roof and guttering the tell tale signs of football activity were there to be interpreted. Lines of hooks that once tethered the goal netting, still stood proud of the former pitch. There was the odd lost football stud, perhaps snagged in a quagmire pitch. There was a line of old coins, pre-decimal of course, that once rained down from the terraces. Not aimed at a cowering goalkeeper but irony of ironies, a ghostly collection to try and save the club. These old pennies and halfpennies fell on deaf ears, silently missing the target of the sheet and instead hitting the goal net and lying unused and never collected, walked into the surrounding cinder track. The pea gravel of the track still showed as blushing pink when exposed once more.

These were mysteries unpicked by the archaeologists with the help of the Park Avenue community that wandered down day after day to monitor the progress of the excavations. The former fans gladly furnished information embellished with wonderful memories. Slicing off that turf took us all back together on an adventure to relive former football glories and of course suffer the many woes of missed opportunities, shots skewed wide of what appeared to be crooked goal posts.

The Bradford community were fascinated by the project and once again the fate of the former league club was debated long and hard. There were tears as well as smiles and laughter as we attempted a re-enactment of the final attacking moves of league football played at the Horton Park End of the ground.

Admission price on exterior wall

Archaeology volunteers Mick Pendleton and Bethan Ward, on the goalmouth dig, 2015

Goal net hook and marker, 2015

Football is of course a very emotional game and so maybe we shouldn't be surprised that some people even reacted with anger at the ruined state of the spiritual home of their now reviving club. For most though it was a week of happy nostalgia and an opportunity to reclaim collective history and memories from the rampages of nature and time.

I kept a daily blog during the project and the guys from Breaking Ground BPA kindly offered to host it. I guess with my Ayresome Park background I ought to have realised how popularly received the progress reports from the dig and artists would be. Yet the project captured everyone's imaginations in a far bigger way than expected. Today I am also a real convert to the Bradford Park Avenue story. There is something very special indeed about this place designed over a century ago by the almost venerated football stadia guru Archibald Leitch, who incidentally also drew up the plans at Ayresome Park. The back to back stand for the football and cricket holds a fascination, our attempts to locate the team dugouts and front of the structure eluded us this time but were followed closely online. Mention the former Dolls House and people's eyes mist over. Almost as if it was an enchanted palace.

Park Avenue was a people's palace. And I hope through our project we have opened up a portal to a 1001 memories but equally also perhaps opened a new chapter for a sports ground with a rich history but also clearly deserving of a future.

As we were scraping away at the soil revealing clues from the past there came the unmistakable sounds of bat on ball from the cricket pitch above us. Then as we put away our trowels at the end of our working day a group of students wandered onto the green sward of the former football pitch carrying an archery target.

One of my special memories was when we played Czechoslovakia, who had just won the Olympics. They played an exhibition match to open the new stadium lights. There were over 17,000 at the game. Avenue lost 3-2 which was not bad. Gibson got one and the other was an own goal. That's the only time we got a bit of luck. Quite frankly we don't get any luck at all. The only other time was in 1961-62 when we got promotion.

The first time I came to Park Avenue was in 1949. All I really remember was the rain. We were playing Preston North End. I was seven and I sat on my father's shoulders. Geoffrey Atack

E260.1 Floodlight bulb from former ground Bradford Park Avenue, 1907
Courtesy National Football Mueseum

The last Archibald Leitch crash barrier

→
Tree: Goat Willow
Scientific name: *Salix caprea*
Alan Ward
Photograph, 2015

Telegraph & Argus

 LAST CITY

No. 31,721 SIXPENCE — BRADFORD, SATURDAY, MAY 30, 1970

THE FAMILY RENDEZVOUS — WIMPY BAR, BROADWAY, BRADFORD. FOR PERFECTION IN EATING.

Lucky Jim in blaze escape

A 15-year-old apprentice had a lucky escape when fire broke out in a small warehouse in East parade, near Barkerend road, Bradford, today.

Jim McGroarty of Woodhead road, Bradford, was looking for a metal frame in the warehouse of W. Dicks, upholsterers. Walter Glass in Barkerend Road who owns the building as a store.

"I could smell burning," said Jim, "and when I looked behind me I could see a fire."

He gave the alarm and other workers rushed across to close the doors to try to prevent it reading.

"It is lucky he wasn't further inside the building," said foreman Mr. Watson Metcalfe. Damage was severe.

Two or three cars had also been stored in the building, known as Scala Garage, for some years and these were badly damaged. It is not known who owns them. The building is Bradford Corporation property.

4 senior police suspended

A chief-superintendent, two inspectors, and a sergeant in the Leeds City police force have been suspended from duty.

Mr. Austin Haywood, Deputy Chief Constable of Leeds, announced today that the suspensions followed a criminal investigation. "The men will appear in court in due course," he said.

LATE NEWS

Cambridge United voted in — big majority against Bradford club

AVENUE GIVEN BOOT BY FOOTBALL LEAGUE

Herbert Metcalfe — we will fight on

From STANLEY PEARSON, CAFE ROYAL, LONDON

BRADFORD (Park Avenue) have been booted out of the Football League and replaced by non-League club Cambridge United.

Avenue won only 17 votes at the League annual meeting at the Cafe Royal, Regent Street, London, compared with 31 for Cambridge.

Member clubs re-elected were Darlington (47 votes), Hartlepool (42) and Newport County (31). Apart from Cambridge's 31 votes the only other non-League club to gain any sort of support was Wigan Athletic with 18.

The news came as a dreadful blow to the Bradford contingent in the packed meeting. The Park Avenue delegation was headed by chairman Herbert Metcalfe, vice-chairman George Sutcliffe, manager Frank Tomlinson and coach Ron Lewin.

The club have been playing at Park Avenue for 63 years. They were seeking re-election for the fourth successive year.

MEETING

The Bradford directors, after they had time to consider the sensational news, said they would hold a board meeting at Park Avenue on Monday night to consider the club's future.

Mr. Metcalfe said: "I am dreadfully disappointed at the result. It was far worse than we had ever expected. I don't think the clubs seeking re-election had their situation put very clearly by the chairman in his remarks prior to the voting.

"We also objected to the way that a spokesman for the third and fourth division clubs, who had wanted to say something about these remarks, was overruled from the chair.

"I don't want to say any more about this matter now until we have had time to consider the full implications."

He added later: "Obviously I am disappointed. I think that the rumpus last October played a big part, but I still think it was right.

"We shall fight on regardless. We may play in the Northern Premier League next season."

SHAKER

Mr. Sutcliffe added: "The shaker of this election for me, apart from our own failure, was the number of votes gained by Newport County. Nothing definite will be decided until the meeting on Monday night."

Mr. Tomlinson admitted that he was shattered by the news.

"It was totally unexpected," he said. "I don't know what the future will hold — we'll have to wait and see."

Mr. Jim Mellor, Bradford City secretary, who was also at the meeting, summing up the feelings of many other clubs, added: "We have had a feeling for a while now that the other clubs would vote the way they have done today. The voting came as not great surprise to me personally."

Cambridge supporters were
Continued on Back Page

Shapely Cambridge United supporters parade in favour of their successful club.

Comment

On this sad day for the faithful who have supported Park Avenue through the last few frustrating seasons leading up to today's departure of the club from the Football League, our first thoughts are for the non-Bradfordian who has fought so hard to keep the club alive.

Many others have preceded Lancastrian Mr. Herbert Metcalfe in the forefront of the battle, but no one has shown such enthusiasm in the face of such long odds, personally committed himself to such a degree.

The long years of arguing the pros and cons of possible Avenue - City merger are now over. It is unfortunate that it has had to be the Football League club and not the city itself, which has made the decision that Bradford is to be a one-club city.

It is, however, no good crying into our football boots; that fund of enthusiasm at Park Avenue, which has been given such a heavy shoulder charge today, should not be allowed to die.

Whatever the future of Park Avenue in whatever sphere, now is the time for the oft-dejected football fans in this area to get their shoulders behind Bradford City and begin the long uphill push into the First Division.

Pink tights to save blushes

The steepness of the 70,000 capacity Jalisco Stadium at Guadalajara, stage for the World Cup finals, has caused a revision of sartorial plans and cost the Mexican organisers 100 pairs of pink tights.

Originally, the group of pretty Mexican girls, assigned to help journalists were equipped with a dress, a pair of shoes, a bag and a lineout—all in pink.

But, climbing the stairs into the Press section behind one of the beauties stopped Press Officer Salazar dead in his tracks.

"Honestly, I could see the white of her neck. There would have been a riot on match day," he gasped.

Accordingly, speedy orders went out for 100 pairs of pink tights for the girls.

Meanwhile, strict warnings against World Cup players using dope were issued today.

A whole team might be thrown out of the championship if any doping allegations are proved, warned Mr. Harry Cavan, a vice-president of the international Federation of Football Associations.

"If we find a player has been doped and we decide there has been connivance with team officials, then that team might find themselves thrown out of the championship," he declared.

The Foreign Minister of Colombia, Senor Alfonso Lopez Michelsen, has sent a message to Britain's Foreign Minister, Mr. Michael Stewart, assuring him there was no "hostility" nor "sport conspiracy" against England in the World Cup championships or against Bobby Moore.

Within a few hours of joining the World Cup squad yesterday, Bobby Moore displayed no signs of ill-ease as England went through a punishing 90-minute training session in temperatures hovering above 100F.

Mexico, as host country, is expected to gross more than £2,500,000 from the event. Although the organising committee said today: "We will not know how much profit we can make until afterwards." Reasonable estimates are that £1,250,000 will go into the local football federation treasury.

 MEXICO 70

Powell issues a new warning

MR. ENOCH POWELL declared today that Commonwealth immigration — "the greatest danger Britain faces" — carries a threat of division, violence and bloodshed of American dimensions.

And he demanded: "Halt immigration now." This is the main point in his election address published today, in which he also warned of two other great dangers "— the Common Market and Socialism."

On the question of joining the six, he promised: "I shall do my utmost to make sure we never do."

And on his third major theme he declared that if the rush into State control continued Britain would cease to be a country where people of initiative wished to live.

Mr. Powell told his electors in Wolverhampton South-West: "The greatest danger Britain faces is Commonwealth immigration and its consequences.

"While this is going on, about 130,000 British-born people emigrate every year. In all our history nothing remotely similar has happened before.

"It carries a threat of division, violence and bloodshed of American dimensions, and adds a powerful weapon to the armoury of anarchy and Socialism."

Mr. Robert Milligan, Government Chief Whip, has been named Anthony Greenwood as Minister of Housing and Local Government.

Mr. Greenwood resigned today on being appointed, with effect from Monday, to the Board of the Commonwealth Development Corporation as prospective chairman on the retirement of Lord Howick in November.

The vacancy of Government Chief Whip is not being filled for the time being.

Speaking at an open air meeting at a new shopping centre on the outskirts of Belper, Derbyshire today Mr. George Brown asked how the Conservatives were going to find the money for their promised £1,500m. tax cuts and £1,000m. in extra expenditure.

Mr. Brown was being officially adopted as Belper's Labour candidate at a private party meeting this afternoon. He had a majority of 4,274 in

---

Anthony Scarfe, aka 'Avenue Arry'
Bradford Park Avenue mascot, 2016

When we got booted out of the football league it was terrible – it was like a knife through your heart, it really was. I will never forget the day. I was sat at home in the front with the radio on because we knew the result was coming. And it came on the radio 'Bradford Park Avenue have been booted out of the football league', I just threw my transistor across the room.

My mother always blamed Park Avenue for me failing my A levels. I was in the middle of taking them and to me, I just could not get my head around it.

Dave (Rolo) Rawling

I believe it was the day after our last match at Valley Parade against Goole Town, which I seem to remember we won one nil in the last minute ... the winding-up meeting was at the Midland Hotel in Bradford. Not much was said there and I can't remember there being many people – maybe 20 or 30. And it was all very formal and over in less then ten minutes. And then people just wandered out and that was it, that was Avenue.

Jeremy Charnock

Gathering for *One Minute Applause* performance

One Minute Applause
Neville Gabie
Video stills, 2015

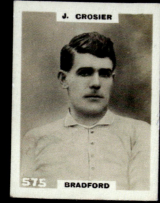

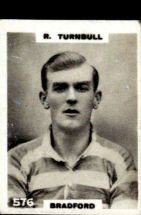

Pinnace cigarette footballer cards, issued by British tobacco company Godfrey Phillips Ltd. in the

Kevin Moore

MUSEUMS OF THE FUTURE

The collections held by the National Football Museum are vast, varied and eclectic. They range from valuable trophies, medals and historic items to the anecdotes and personal memorabilia many football fans would have in personal collections. The challenge is how to reinterpret this material in new and interesting ways. One method, very evident in the *Breaking Ground* project is to work with artists and see how they might bring a different perspective to what is our national sport.

I first met Neville Gabie soon after he published his very successful book POSTS [Penguin 1999], a collection of his photographs of informal goalposts found around the world. That and his other arts/football commissions in Middlesbrough and with Liverpool Football Club Museum suggested that he might be one such artist that would bring something fresh to our displays. It was Neville who suggested working with the archaeologist and sports historian Jason Wood at Bradford Park Avenue. With additional funding from the Arts Council, they developed a project involving a range of other artists and academics and fans; an archaeological dig of parts of the former football ground and of the goalpost holes at the Horton Park end of the ground. As far as I am aware, something entirely unique in relation to football.

The National Football Museum is always looking to engage with new audiences and extend the reach with 'offsite' projects well beyond Manchester. Once again *Breaking Ground* did exactly that. In 2013 and again in 2015 a team of artists and archaeologists with the blessing of Bradford Metropolitan Council spent several days working onsite on the former football ground, with full access to all members of the public. In addition to the numerous fans of Park Avenue who turned up to help and share their stories, several school groups and members of the public were given tours of the 'dig' and the terraces. As the event took place during the National Science Festival in Bradford, a team of Bradford University staff and students also contributed to the project doing a full geophysical survey of the site and introducing their working methods and technology to members of the public. This multi-disciplinary approach is part of the richness of the *Breaking Ground* experience.

My vision for the future is that we continue to use our collection as a resource for artists, writers, academics, ordinary fans and members of the public to interpret and enjoy. Equally I would like to think that the National Football Museum can continue to work right across the country in a range of 'offsite' projects, with the museum in Manchester being the hub and springboard for that activity.

Dr Kevin Moore
Director
National Football Museum

Artist biographies

Neville Gabie completed an MA in Sculpture at the Royal College of Art, London in 1988. Key to his practice is a sustained engagement with place and community in a range of contexts from the remoteness of an Antarctic Research station [British Antarctic Survey] to a two year residency on the London Olympic Park during construction. A passionate football fan, he has worked on several projects that combine football and art. These include *Trophy Room*, a public art commission on Ayresome Park, Middlesbrough, former home ground of Middlesbrough FC; and *Posts*, an on-going collection of photographs of improvised goalposts found around the world published by Penguin Books. These have been exhibited widely, including at three World Cups, the FIFA Headquarters and the Tokyo Metropolitan Museum of Photography. He is currently working on a major commission with Alan Ward for Cambridge City Council celebrating the first written rules for football in the modern era. His work is included in the Tate Gallery and Arts Council Collections and collections in South Africa | www.nevillegabie.com

Chris Gaffney leads the School of Archaeological Sciences at the University of Bradford. He was appointed to the staff at Bradford in October 2007 but his link with the University goes back to the 1980s where he undertook his undergraduate and postgraduate degrees. Having completed his doctoral research, Chris formed (with John Gater) GBS Prospection, a commercial archaeological geophysical company which became the largest group working in Britain. In the summer of 2007 Chris was awarded an Honorary Doctorate for popularising archaeological geophysics via Channel 4's *Time Team* programme and other media opportunities. He is the current Editor of the journal *Archaeological Prospection* and the past Chair of the International Society for Archaeological Prospection.

Robert Nichols has been a Boro fan all of his life. In fact he's not missed a Middlesbrough game home or away since September 1999 when his brother got married in Hong Kong. He has edited the Boro fanzine *Fly Me To The Moon* for 25 years or so. Although Rob also manages the fmttm.com Boro fan website and message board he is commited to keeping the fanzine a printed paper publication. Rob lives on the site of Middlesbrough's former ground Ayresome Park where they almost replicated Bradford Park Avenue, narrowly avoiding complete liquidation by only eight minutes in 1986. He has wielded a trowel on archaeology sites for over 30 years and hopes one day soon to excavate at Ayresome Park.

Louise O'Reilly is an illustrator and educator whose work includes drawing, painting, artist's books and surface design. She studied History of Art at Winchester School of Art and Birkbeck College, London before training in Illustration at Oxford and Cherwell College, the Society of Botanical Artists and the University of Cambridge Botanical Gardens. Her creative work starts with observational drawing and is inspired by scientific and natural history illustration. As an amateur naturalist she is always keen to explore the nearest green space from derelict urban sites to highly cultivated historic gardens. She regularly provides short courses for clients such as Capel Manor College, Tate, Forty Hall and the National Trust. After 10 years in a mixed design studio in East London she moved to Suffolk in 2016 to take on the creative challenge of secondary school art teaching.

Oliver Palmer and **Giorgio Garippa**'s collaborative practice began at Oxford Brookes University in 2006 with the project, *Shelter* (2006-2010). Realised across three incarnations, the project engaged them in a critical approach that allowed them to consolidate their research whilst keeping it fluid.
Having developed their individual practices with Masters' degrees from Goldsmiths (Oliver, 2013) and Wimbledon College of Arts (Giorgio, 2013), their collaborative team has now been reunited through several new projects and residencies. With Oliver influenced by the neo-avant-gardes and Giorgio by Italian Neorealism, their practices blend to an eclectic unity.
They each bring skills that allow the practice to inhabit sound, video, photography, drawing, sculpture and installation. Through the use of recovered materials they examine the processes that constitute our sense of identity and of how historical, environmental, social, economic and political experiences shape and reflect our desires and experiences of the spaces we inhabit.

David Pendleton is one of Bradford's leading historians of sport and leisure. The grounds at Park Avenue featured heavily in his PhD thesis *Sport and the Victorian City: The development of commercialised spectator sport, Bradford 1836-1908*. Although David is often linked with Avenue's neighbours Bradford City, his first ever football game was actually Avenue's last ever Football League victory. David was taken by his Avenue supporting father to witness a 3-0 victory over Hartlepool United in March 1970. After Avenue folded in 1974 David's family gravitated towards Valley Parade and he has been a keen supporter of the Bantams ever since. His two books *Glorious 1911* and *Paraders, the 125 year history of Valley Parade* were best sellers at Waterstones with the latter receiving the dubious accolade of being the most stolen book over Christmas 2011. David was *Breaking Ground*'s historical consultant and ad hoc tour guide during the excavations at Park Avenue in September 2015.

Alan Ward is an artist and designer based in Manchester, and is known for his book design and publishing collaborations with artists. His personal photographic projects are based around the subject of place and include: *Citizen Manchester*, a two year artist residency at Manchester Central Library during its refurbishment; *Costumbre* (ritual); and *Chateau Series I & II*, the latter resulting in a publication with poet Helen Tookey entitled *Telling the Fractures*. Alan is a die-hard Norwich fan. He is currently re-imagining an early 20th century photographer's rediscovered archive and is co-artist on cambridgerules1848.com | alanjward.co.uk

Jason Wood has been an archaeologist and heritage consultant for over 35 years and Director of Heritage Consultancy Services since 1998. His other posts have included Professor of Cultural Heritage at Leeds Metropolitan University, Head of Heritage at WS Atkins Consultants Limited and Assistant Director of Lancaster University Archaeological Unit. He was Chairman of the National Trust's Archaeology Panel for nine years until 2014, and has played an influential role in the affairs of other heritage organisations such as the Chartered Institute for Archaeologists, the Royal Institution of Chartered Surveyors, the International Council on Monuments and Sites UK and UNESCO. Jason is an elected member of a number of professional institutions and a Fellow of the Society of Antiquaries of London.

Supporters and subscribers to *Breaking Ground*

Alan Bean
Roger Banks
Peter Barker
Phillip Bates
Bradford Park Avenue Supporters Club
Dennis Brickley
David Brigg
Keith Bonney
Stephen Brook
Mark Brookes
Ian Brown
Gordon Buchanan
Bill Byford
Ella Byford
Denise Campbell
Jeremy Charnock
Tim Clapham
Tony Clegg
John AW Clough
Stephen Connell
Dominic Cummings
Gordon Cummings
Philip Daynes
Susan Davies (nee Barraclough)
Keith Denison
David Dyson
Paul Dyson
Dave Ellyatt
Stephen Exley
Howard Fricker
Dean Gardner
Mason Gardner
Kevin Haley
Steven Haigh
Peter Holden
David Horrill
Trevor Hutchinson
Simon Inglis

Brian Jeeves
Bill Jones
Callum Keating
Graham Lee
Audrey Lewis
John Mawson
Dominic McKenzie, Sale
Allan Mirfield
Joe Mosley
Susan Naylor and June Hendry (nee Farr)
Tony Niland
Peter Oversby
David Pendleton
Mick Pendleton
Rosie Pendleton
Andrew D Pickles
Andrew Pinfield
Gareth Roberts
Dave (Rolo) Rawling
John Rawnsley
Andrew Rishworth
Lewis Sale
Mike Stead
Dave Stordy
Robert Stott
John Sucksmith
Brian Sutcliffe
Paul Town Stadium Portraits
Danny Ward
Paul Waterhouse
Stephen Waterhouse
Brent Whittam
Lynda Wilkinson
Alan Wintersgill
Phil Wood, Kingston Ontario
Pete Zemroch

Acknowledgements

This project would not have been as rewarding without the passionate enthusiasm of Bradford Park Avenue's many fans. Their extensive knowledge, wonderful stories and the memorabilia they shared with us has been key to the project's success. So our first thanks are to all those fans.

Breaking Ground began with a desire to literally 'dig' into the football past of the site using traditional archaeology and more contemporary geophysical technology. Our thanks go to the staff and students of Bradford University who offered their time and expertise. In particular Chris Gaffney, Thomas Sparrow, Danielle Farrar, and Sam Dollman. Also to Mick Pendleton, David Pendleton, Rob Nichols, and to all those volunteers who came for a day, or a couple of hours to help with the dig.

Although there has been a limited amount of funding, our ambitions for the project vastly exceeded what we had. The production of this wonderful book has relied almost entirely on the expertise, goodwill and commitment of Alan Ward and his son Sebastian Ward. It is just as well they are both huge football fans. Also to Stuart Hewetson-Ward (no relation) for filming onsite and for assembling the DVD. Thanks also to Linda Dunn and Ben East for reading and proofing the final drafts, and also to Bill Davis and Herman Minne at Graphius Group for their advice and help with the print production.

The project was initiated with funding from the National Football Museum and Arts Council England, and led by Neville Gabie and Jason Wood. A further Grants for the Arts application by Neville Gabie, with match funding from the National Football Museum, allowed us to expand our project in 2015 and to invite additional participants. We were joined by David Pendleton, bringing his extensive historic knowledge of the Victorian sports heritage in Bradford to the project; Rob Nichols supporting the archaeology; artists Louise O'Reilly, Alan Ward, Oliver Palmer and Giorgio Garippa. Thanks to all those above who helped in showing school groups and visitors around the old ground, in addition to making their own work onsite.

The former ground is owned by Bradford Metropolitan Council. Without their support in giving us access, we would not have been able to proceed. Thanks in particular to Phil Barker, Mick Priestley and Bobsie Robinson for their willingness to help us.

The National Football Museum has a vision to involve artists in telling the story of our national game and in extending the museum's reach beyond the building. Thanks to Kevin Moore, Andy Pearce and John O'Shea for this vision and for supporting our endeavour.

Neville Gabie and Jason Wood

Image credits

Unless otherwise stated all photography is by the authors and artists.

Archaeological plans: B. Nilgun Oz

Archaeological finds photography: Loura Conerney, Daca Studio

National Football Museum p. 31

The memorabilia was photographed during the open days at the Park Avenue dig in 2015 and also during a photography drop-in weekend in 2016 at the current ground.
The publishers have made every effort to identify or trace copyright holders but apologise for any omissions that may have been made inadvertently.

Peter Barker p. 1, 10, 42, 46, 104, 120, 122, 131, 152

Keith Bonney p. 140

Stephen Brook p. 115

Tim Clapham p. 22, 26, 90 (photo), 116, 118, 122, 126, 141

Keith Denison p. 9, 14, 150

Tom Hiland p. 25, 36, 94, 112, 121,

Graham Lee p. 130

Allan Mirfield p. 91

Susan Naylor & Julie Hendry (nee Farr) p. 11, pp. 85–86, pp. 88, 89

David Pendleton p. 20, 138

Andrew Pinfield p. 113

Jan Richards (medal) p. 90

Mike Stead p. 13

John Sucksmith p. 28, 47, 123, 124

Front endpapers: photographic collage created from fan memorabilia supplied by Peter Oversby

Rear endpapers: from programmes supplied by Graham Lee and Keith Denison

DVD disk artwork taken from programme cover supplied by Graham Lee

Our thanks also to John Rawnsley and Peter Holden for sharing their collections and memories.

The Bradford (Park Avenue) Remembered Facebook community has also been a helpful and friendly resource.

Kick-off 3-15

Kick-off 3-15

Kick-off 3-15

Official Programme PRICE 2ᴰ·
Kick-off 3-15

Official Programme PRICE 2ᴰ·
Kick-off 3-15

Kick-off 3-15

Kick-off 3-15

Official Programme PRICE 2ᴰ·
Kick-off 3-15

Official Programme PRICE 2ᴰ·

Officia